James Kingham

HOW TO BECOME A STARTUP PRO "ON THE SIDE"

BOOK 1

© 2019 James Kingham

All rights reserved.

This book may not be published in whole or part, stored in a retrieval system, or transmitted in any form or by any means electronic, mechanical or other without written permission from the author or appropriate agents. Reviewers may quote brief passages.

ACKNOWLEDGEMENTS

To my family and friends for their understanding about the missed hours spent getting all of this stuff down on paper.

To myself, it's my book after all so why not take the opportunity to blow my own trumpet a little? As it turns out, the struggle of writing is just one element of successfully completing a book. Like many creators I struggle to consciously override my addictive and often magpie like nature, whilst ignoring the overwhelming and often all consuming need to chase perfection. For that accomplishment alone my creative self deserves a shout out.

To my sister, who helped my family at a very difficult time in my life. I can never repay her in a way that would represent my gratitude for what she did, so this dedication is my small way of saying thank you.

To my partner for her undying enthusiasm for everything I do. Even when that involves me whittling on about new ideas in the early hours or running my latest empire building schemes by her at the most inopportune moments. She is a master at making boredom and desperation look positively engaging and interesting.

To my long gone Grandparents for their never-ending support of my hair brained schemes, crazy ideas, and entrepreneurial ventures. Their unconditional support allowed my confidence, natural curiosity and independence to grow and flourish.

To my dad, who's less than traditional approach to child rearing made resourcefulness, self preservation, independence and standing on your own two feet mandatory. For the development of those qualities alone, I guess the old man did an ok job.

To the many mentors, coaches and teachers I have had the pleasure to work alongside over the years. Your teachings continue to change lives today.

And finally to my editor Kim of the writing surgery for her tireless work in deciphering my brain dump madness into something that actually resembles a reasonable body of work. Kim can be contacted at the writingsurgery.com

DEDICATION

This Book is dedicated to the army of creative everyday entrepreneurs who stop talking about how great their ideas are and actually start making them happen. In the words of Freddy Mercury and Queen "You make the rocking world go round".

"Success does not happen by itself, it does however love a defined plan, unbreakable commitment and consistent action"- James Kingham

Contents

Acknowledgements 3
Dedication...5
About The Author 10
Need Some Help? 11
We Are All Born Entrepreneurs.................................12
Before We Start 16
So Why Did I Write This Book?.................................19
The Startup Universe 25
In The Beginning..29
The Young Entrepreneur.......................................33
A Cunning Plan..41
The Mighty Fall..55
Ashes & The Phoenix 57
The Inevitability Of Change 62
Why, Why & Why?...65
Getting Started..66
What's Your Freedom?..72
You're a Scientist...74
You Don't Need A YES 76
Learn Once, Apply Many 78
Concept To Cash 80
Learn The Rules Of The Game 82

The Practice Of Learning	85
Mastery - SHU-HA-RI	87
Don't Underestimate Your Value	91
Sink Your Biggest Competitor	94
Cost Vs Investment	98
Ideas Need Action	101
Get A Teacher	105
Define Important	108
Simplicity Breeds Effectiveness	111
Define, Develop & Deliver	114
Launch & Test Your MVP	118
Learn To Listen	120
Expect To Pivot	121
Risk Is Unavoidable	122
Minimising Your ETR	124
Plan, But Not Too Much	128
Ditch Your Excuses	129
Clarity & Vision	131
Be Specific	133
Move Your Mountains	135
Keep To The Deadline	136
Keep Focused On The Finish Line	137
Don't Play It Safe	139

Comfort Is Not Your Friend 141

Fear The Highwayman 142

Getting Quick Results 147

Don't Wait For Approval 151

It's Got To Be Perfect 152

Master The 80/20 Rule 154

Learn While You Earn 156

The Hidden Accelerator 157

Laziness, The Hidden Asset 159

Stand Up & Stand Out 161

Deliver On The Promise 168

Take Your Seat At The Table 170

Value Your Time 172

Leverage Your IP 173

Customer Creation 176

Boosting Productivity 181

Turning On The Autopilot 183

Scaling Your Income 188

Get In Touch 198

About The Author

Based in the UK, James Kingham (aka *"The Online Startup Pro"*) is a coach, mentor and trainer who calls upon his twenty five years of successful commercial experience to help new entrepreneurs, creators and professional practitioners to develop and launch successful startup businesses.

James is the author of several best selling startup books, writes for a number of industry journals, blogs and forums, alongside speaking and presenting at business events, seminars and exhibitions.

James loves to hear about your *"on the side"* startup experiences and often shares stories and does follow up interviews, so why not get in touch and let him know what you have created and he will happily share your story.

james@onlinestartuppro.com

www.onlinestartuppro.com

Need Some Help?

Do you need help launching your startup, new venture, project, department or enterprise?

Do you want to discover how to implement an effective startup culture within your organisation?

Do you want to learn how to define, develop and implement lean and agile startup practices that create unbeatable differentiation for your business?

Do you want to be able to create effective automated marketing platforms and systems that deliver sustainable competitive advantage?

Then why not join thousands of like-minded entrepreneurs and signup for my startup pros newsletter and get access to a wealth of free resources, training, help and expertise to help you get started.

www.onlinestartuppro.com

We Are All Born Entrepreneurs

It's a sad fact of life that the majority of wannabe entrepreneurs will never get to fulfil their lifelong ambitions, dreams and aspirations of becoming successful startup owners. Many will spend their valuable time talking about doing it but will fail to take the action needed to actually make it happen, whilst others will only ever muster a token *"have a go"* gesture but will rarely commit with enough *"all in"* effort to cross the finish line successfully.

Unfortunately for the growing army of wannabe entrepreneurial freedom fighters and soon to be *"billionaire business tycoons"* they often find themselves held back by their own lack of self-confidence, limiting beliefs and the constrained mindsets that have built up over the years. They will often focus on and listen to negative narratives, associate with the wrong types of influencers and continue to be guided and often misled by others. More often than not they believe that *"success"* is what happens to other people and deep down don't believe that they too have the skills, knowledge and expertise to become successful *"on the side"* startup entrepreneurs.

For those of you out there having doubts about your ability to make it as an *"on the side"* startup entrepreneur, I'm going to demonstrate how you already possess all the qualities and attributes needed to turn your dreams into a reality. The biggest stumbling block for many new startup founders is not, as many believe, a lack of ideas, finances or resources. The real challenge is that their true and natural entrepreneurial spirit has become dumbed down and buried over the years by the ongoing drudgery of day-to-day habits, routines and behaviours. This situation is further exacerbated by the overwhelming compliance to think, act and conform to the traditional rules and role models that others have defined.

The truth is, *we are all born entrepreneurs*, salespeople and expert marketeers. In fact we are naturally born that way and learn to hone those skills early on in order to survive. Don't believe me? Simply take a look at any child. Children are masters of the entrepreneurial craft. They are highly skilled sales people who deliver compelling pitches, create irresistible offers and are experts at removing obstacles, solving problems and reframing their proposals. Every child also has the uncanny knack of maximising emotional hooks, they are never afraid to ask for the sale, and will unashamedly use every psychological trick in the book to close the deal. Now that sounds like all of the ingredients needed to become a first-class entrepreneur to me. I know from experience that my own children, and those of others for that matter, have sold me time and time again and that's with an intimate knowledge of how this stuff works. My advice for budding entrepreneurs follows that of the great Jim Rohn:

"Think like a child."

From a young age I was always curious about the mechanics of how things worked, and this curiosity naturally led me to start up a number of small *"on the side"* enterprises over the years. I grew them, overcame unforeseen challenges, navigated the inevitable ups and downs and had a fair degree of success, even if it was on a very small scale at that time. What's important to understand here is that these early successes were achieved without the benefits of any real-life experiences, soft skills, business education, training or access to the mass of free online resources that are available today. The point is I set up my own little enterprises out of sheer necessity and ran them on nothing more than pure instinct and gut feel. I was not following a grand plan or trying to replicate anyone else's successes. I just got up and did what needed to be done in order to deliver the desired outcome. In many cases my simplistic child-like thinking and resourcefulness was, as it turned out, all I needed to succeed.

When we are young, unencumbered and carefree, everything seems uncomplicated and achievable. We don't care too much about rejection, politics or spending time reasoning why or how failure is so inevitable, we just tend to knuckle down and get on with it, happy to experiment, fail and learn as we go. You would think that with age and wisdom alongside the benefits of hindsight, experience and education that it would be easier to navigate the complexities of getting a startup project successfully off the ground. The reality however is very different. With time, knowledge and experience comes belief, emotion and complexity, whereby we appear to lose our natural born talents, curiosity and the ability to think, and more importantly act, with the same freedom we did as children. Remember that simplistic view of the world where anything and everything was possible, and where failure had little or no consideration or consequences in your plans? Back to the real world and this way of thinking seems to have vanished into a cynical quagmire of opinionated views, immovable perceptions and self-limiting beliefs that continually serve to restrict our actions.

We are all born as free thinkers and resourceful problem solvers, in fact our very survival depends upon it. The challenge facing most of us in today's modern society however is that we have become accustomed to being constantly spoon-fed, directed and told what to do, when to do it and how. It's this fundamentally flawed command and control mindset that's been slowly eroding our true natural resourcefulness down the generations. But here is the good news. It's simple to get that resourcefulness back and to start thinking like a child again.

You can start doing this quickly by implementing a *"simple thinking"* strategy into your everyday life by choosing to take a child-like view of situations, problems and dilemmas. Challenge everything, start using language like *"why"*, *"what if"* and *"why not"*. Train yourself to strip away the complex, simplify everything and start seeing things for what and how they really are rather than what you are told they should be. Take a single-minded approach and be mindful not to become adversely influenced, controlled or manipulated by others. Be open with your views but bloody minded and unmovable when it comes to execution and application. Whenever you find yourself lost in complexity, or your thinking starts to become limited or biased by your limiting beliefs, just take ten seconds out and ask how your six-year-old self would approach the situation. Apply this simple practice routinely for several weeks and you will be amazed by how simple and possible everything suddenly starts to look again.

Before We Start

As this may be the first time you have heard of me and are probably thinking, *"Who the hell is this guy?"* I thought I would take this opportunity to tell you a little bit about myself, my background and why I put the proverbial pen to paper and wrote this book.

My name is James Kingham and I class myself as an *"on the side"* multipreneur; that is I have developed a portfolio of side businesses projects and interests that contribute to my annual income. Like many of you reading this I have worked within traditional employment roles over the years, including contracting, freelancing and consulting. I have done this while at the same time starting a variety of successful *"on the side"* micro business projects in my spare time. I say *"spare time"* but that's not strictly true because no time is truly *"spare"*, it's either *productively invested time* or *leisure time,* but more on that topic later. Let's just say that I committed to reserve some of my time and wisely invested it for the purposes of developing additional income streams that would provide me the finances, time and freedom I needed to develop the kind of lifestyle I desired.

After many years of starting successful on the side **"micro businesses"** I have taken everything I have learned and distilled it down into a simple process that I have come to call **QSS** or **Quick, Small and Simple.** The QSS startup framework largely follows lean and agile principles and allows me to quickly recognise opportunities and then define, develop and deliver products and services to meet those unmet demands effectively.

I now run, invest in and co-own a number of diverse ventures including book publishing, business consultancy, electrical contractors, a personal development and coaching business for elite performers, a premium confectionery store and several thriving online enterprises. The thing is, I am certainly not an expert in all of these areas but I have partnered with people who are. I have simply trained myself to quickly identify opportunities where things could be done differently, improved upon, made cheaper, faster, more convenient, more accessible or more exciting. I then engineer simple *"soft"* innovative ways to solve those problems. Later in the book I will share with you how I applied a really simple innovative twist to a mundane commodity product that gave me an instant advantage over every single competitor within that market. And the best bit, it didn't cost me a penny.

One thing I will tell you before we get started is this: I'm just like many of you reading this book. I wanted to develop enough independent financial security to release my time, gain more freedom and remove my reliance upon others for my primary source of income. I simply developed an effective and systemised process to make that happen.

Unlike many, I do not profess to be some kind of guru. I certainly still have a mountain of lessons to learn and, unfortunately or fortunately depending upon your perspective, continue to do so on a far too regular basis. When all's said and done *I can only tell you what I know* and if that helps you to get started, improves upon or motivates you on your own entrepreneurial journey then I will have succeeded with the purpose of this book.

As you read this book you will notice a certain amount of overlap within some areas alongside a degree of continued repetition where I appear to labour on certain points. This approach follows that of a simple military training method.

Telling them what you're going to tell them.

Tell them.

Tell them what you told them.

In short, the recurring points and repetition are important and necessary and as such should be embedded within your own approach.

So Why Did I Write This Book?

Many startup gurus, books and new entrepreneurs themselves for that matter often focus on the big startup vision. This normally involves grand plans of heading up a large venture capital funded industry disruptor that will quickly redefine entire industries or generate completely new markets, with notions of becoming the next Facebook, Airbnb or Uber before being acquired for a gazillion dollars. Whilst having BHAGs (Big Hairy Arsed Goals) for your startup is great from an aspirational perspective, the reality for most entrepreneurs is a whole lot more down to earth. In my experience, what most new entrepreneurs really want is to be able to develop small on the side projects, boutique businesses or solo practices that can augment or replace their current incomes in order to increase freedom, choice and discretionary time. They also want to become accountable for their own security rather than being at the mercy of others for a paycheck. In essence this book is for you, *the everyday "on the side" entrepreneur.*

Big startups, and most start off way too big by the way, take lots of time, effort and money. They can be all consuming, are fraught with risk and have frightening rates of failure. Let's be honest here. You don't really want the hassle, worry and uncertainty of a startup. What you want are quick and easy ways to generate income under your own steam and on your own terms. The best way to do that from a startup perspective is by developing and launching your own portfolio of small discrete micro startups. Micro startups are small simple ideas that can be quickly developed into robust sustainable income streams. The beauty of the micro startup approach lies in its simplicity, speed of setup and income generation capability, whilst keeping investment, uncertainty and risk to an absolute minimum. The second, and some would say greatest, advantage of the micro startup is that you don't have to bet the bank on them. Quitting your job and going *"all in"* on an unknown quantity is a high-risk proposition that's tantamount to gambling. What a micro startup enables you to do is to take your ideas and get started in a small risk-free and fun way. If it works, great, scale it like mad; if it doesn't, scrap it and move on to the next opportunity. It sounds simple and it is, so long as you keep it that way.

As you're reading this book you're probably the type of person who already has a number of great startup ideas and a burning desire and passion to share them with the world. You're probably not afraid of commitment and hard work and are willing to do whatever it takes to make it happen, but for some reason real success is still eluding you, and you're not getting the results you desired or expected. Perhaps you have even ended up working longer hours and in some cases are earning less money. So what went wrong? The most challenging obstacle facing new entrepreneurs is simple. It's the knowledge and ability to get started the smart way.

This book is not intended to be some kind of a staunch prescriptive step by step startup methodology. My approach is far more descriptive in nature, whereby I provide you with simple ideas, actionable strategies, and guidance about starting **Quick, Small and Simple** micro businesses on the side based upon your own specific requirements. I also wanted to share my own experiences, knowledge and expertise of setting up the systems and processes I have used to start producing *fast results*.

Like all entrepreneurs I have made a ton of mistakes along the way. I have had my fair share of failures or *"opportunities to learn"* as they are romantically labelled, but I have also had some great successes along the way. The truth is, you absolutely need the failures to build the experience, resistance and determination required to fuel the successes. In the real world of the startup few get it right the first, second or even the third time around and the best lessons are those learned from rolling up your sleeves and doing it yourself.

> **Startup Pro Insight**: Other people's experience, knowledge and advice (including mine) are great, but nothing keeps you focused and teaches you more than screwing up and falling on your own arse from time to time.

For the parents among you, starting a business is a little like raising children, in that it's a massive undertaking fraught with challenges, obstacles and unexpected events and best of all, it comes without a manual. As with parenting, everyone you know, and some you don't, will have an opinion about how best to achieve success. Advice, anecdotes and theories will be forthcoming by the bucket load, even from those who have never done it personally. There also comes a time when you have no choice but to let your vulnerable baby startup go out into the big wide world and fend for itself. Just as with parenting all you can do is provide enough support and wisdom to minimise the risk of them damaging themselves too much in the process.

Whilst the main focus of this book is business startups, most of the strategies, principles and insights are completely portable and can therefore be adapted and used for just about any type of project you care to mention. My aim is to get you up and running as quickly as possible and actually launch something that customers will pay for. Look at my Startup Pro series of books as a friendly advisory hand on your shoulder as you set out on your entrepreneurial startup journey.

There are so many opportunities out there it's easy .....if you know how.

This is book one of three in the *"How To Become A Startup Pro - On The Side"* series and has been written as a direct result of my own hands-on work, experiences and knowledge gained from twenty-five years of building and launching micro startup businesses. Many of these have been *"on the side"* projects which have been started alongside traditional employment. As it turns out I know a thing or two about how to do it pretty well and now spend a portion of my time advising and helping organisations, institutions and individuals to develop the capability needed to do it successfully. I hope you enjoy the book and you end up realising that getting something successfully launched and becoming a startup pro *"on the side"* is far easier than you ever thought possible.

> **Startup Pro Insight**: All startups, no matter what they provide, to whom or how, have one thing in common. They all need to solve a problem that delivers so much value that their target customers will happily pay for it. The bigger the problem, the bigger the reward.

"Unselfishly helping people get what they want is the quickest way I know of getting what you want." - Jim Rohn

Part I
The Startup Revolution

The Startup Universe

We live in a changing world where just about everyone wants to be starting something. We have evolved into a generation of savvy entrepreneurs, business owners and empire builders, who can bootstrap their startups with nothing more than a simple idea, a meagre self-funded budget and a bucket load of effort and hustle.

Technology has made that easier still by lowering the barriers of entry and accelerating the ability to quite literally get started in an instant. Getting a new venture up and running on the side is now easier, cheaper and more accessible than ever before. This increasing simplicity has had the beneficial impact of enabling the masses of eager "wannapreneurs" to tentatively dip their toes into the dark murky waters of business ownership, self-reliance and entrepreneurial freedom, with ease.

Nowadays, the entrepreneurial spirit is everywhere. It's no longer the remit of the lone isolated maverick disruptor or inventor. Today's entrepreneurs can be found across a diverse range of social types, classes and industries. From specialist consultancies, mums running table top businesses between school runs, right the way through to revolutionary fintechs, exclusive personal trainers, raw food specialists and everything in between. Think of just about any niche or micro niche and chances are there's a group of entrepreneurs out there leveraging the opportunity right now.

Entrepreneurialism is not just the playground of the lifestyle *"freedom seeker"*. We also have a thriving world of *"intrapreneurs"* who are driving the entrepreneurial spirit, culture and thinking right to the heart of the companies they work for. Intrapreneurs are the champions and evangelists of the businesses that employ them and are no less effective than their solo entrepreneurial cousins. They build their own personal brands, create assets, build intellectual property and become industry influencers, providing serious products and service offerings that are highly sought after within their chosen markets. Initially that was exactly the route I took and it's a position that has continued to organically grow and evolve into a number of lucrative diversified business interests.

We live in exciting times where anyone with an idea, a bit of hustle and effort can jump into the rapids of business ownership, steer their own ship and achieve greatness along the way. But, and of course there is always a but, there are rules to the game. These rules are the strategies, principles and lessons that, once learned, will not only make your startup journey a much easier ride but will ensure you have more fun along the way. And please remember above all else, this stuff is supposed to be fun. Why else do it?

In today's dynamic economy, more and more people are moving away from, or in some cases being pushed out of, traditional employment into more exciting entrepreneurial environments. These new entrepreneurs are quickly learning to adapt by abandoning perceived job security and the ageing practices of humdrum corporate nine-to-five existences. They are eagerly seeking more exciting but often more unpredictable paths where the lure of freedom and choice count for much more than just a hefty paycheck.

Even the stalwart and monolithic legacy businesses are slowly realising that the inflexible working practices of old are no longer tenable in the new fast-paced digital world. Attracting talented resources and constraining them to siloed existences within rigid, and often restrictive, organisational confines is becoming much harder to do as the landscape of how and where we choose to work continues to radically shift.

Power in the marketplace is rapidly tipping back in favour of *"intellectual creators"* and those who have the skills, knowledge and experience to solve the most critical challenges faced by businesses. The new entrepreneurial breed is quickly evolving from easily replaceable commodity resources into well informed, sought after business service providers, leveraging their own personal brands, intellectual property and commercial assets.

Flexibility, dynamic lifestyle and freedom have quickly become the entrepreneur's currency of choice. Today's entrepreneurs know their value in the marketplace. They know what they want and more importantly they are learning how to achieve it. Perspectives have altered and working practices have evolved. Over the last ten years we have become far more educated about how to develop independence by working for ourselves, becoming more self-sufficient and designing lifestyles that complement our individuality, talents and desire for freedom.

Enlightened entrepreneurs and forward-thinking proactive businesses know that relationships nowadays have to be ones of collaboration, contribution and co-creation, where achieving common goals and delivering holistic equitable value is the only productive outcome. The old restrictive employee and employer relationships are quickly diminishing. Today these engagements are much more like traditional business to business relationships, where each entity forms part of a cohesive interdependent network that relies upon each other to deliver enhanced customer value.

In future those with valuable subject matter expertise, experience and knowledge will build their own personal brands as businesses. They will no longer maintain monogamous relationships with one employer, but will instead deliver their value and expertise to any number of different organisations and this is an area where many significant opportunities can be found for the army of budding entrepreneurs out there today.

What are you waiting for, really? I hope it's not to be picked or for someone else's approval?

In The Beginning

My first exposure to and experience of entrepreneurialism and that way of thinking and operating was a complete accident. At just ten years old I was already an avid small-time *"on the side"* entrepreneur, although I didn't know it at the time of course. At the tender age of ten I barely had a concept of what life was about other than tearing around on bikes, go-karting, camping in the woods and what time I had to be home for dinner, let alone what entrepreneurs were or, even more mystifyingly, what they did.

Back in the late 1970s and early 80s things were very different. Back then traditional business monoliths ruled the world and most ordinary folk worked for them in one capacity or another. The secret world of the mysterious maverick entrepreneur outliers who lived, thrived and survived outside of *"traditional"* employment models did so by a different set of rules and were most definitely the exception rather than the rule. The exciting and vibrant life of an entrepreneur was a world that most *"normal'* working-class people had little or no knowledge or experience of personally.

As a curious and fresh faced ten-year-old I had no concept or notion of intentionally becoming an entrepreneur. I was not trying to fulfil some mythical vision of following in my entrepreneurial idol's footsteps or reaching the heady heights of becoming a millionaire or even billionaire tycoon. No, I'm afraid it was a lot less sexy than that, where I was from. What I was doing, I was doing simply out of good old-fashioned necessity. Invention, imagination and resourcefulness were all I had to work with at that point in time and as lessons learned years later would reveal it was all I really needed. So that leads me nicely onto how I became an accidental *"on the side"* entrepreneur at the age of just ten and three quarters.

Back then my grandparents would regularly come to visit me and my siblings on Wednesday afternoons after school. They would always bring heavily laden bags filled to the brim with a fine selection of cakes, biscuits and confectionery loveliness. I vividly remember busily saving my meagre pocket money allowance to buy a range of second-hand electronic parts for a robot which I had designed and was building at the time. Even as a youngster I was a bit of a creator and inventor. Back in those *"good ole days",* they weren't good by the way, money was not in great supply. Well, let me expand on that a little, my supply of it was not great and my parents wasted no time in making it very clear that this situation was not likely to change for me any time soon from their perspective. With that qualified it was obvious to me that if I needed money I would have to find inventive and legal(ish) ways of acquiring it myself. At the time that seemed harsh, but in hindsight it taught me an extremely valuable lesson that I have adhered to ever since.

> **Startup Pro Insight:** The only way to achieve anything is to rely only upon yourself to go out and get it. Once you accept this simple truth everything becomes so much clearer and easier to achieve.

Not only does that attitude develop independence and accountability, it also puts you in total control and keeps things really simple. I looked at it this way. If I'm the only one responsible and accountable for making something happen (or not), whatever I want is only ever down to me to go out and achieve. So basically everything is totally within my own control. Now that's an easy concept to grasp and one that changed the game for me in the long term.

Although I didn't know it then, I had a common startup challenge. I had a definite lack of financial resources. The only option in my mind to counter this unfortunate financial predicament I found myself in was to put my **resourcefulness** to work and come up with some funding options of my own.

> **Startup Pro Insight:** A valuable lesson I learned early was that a lack of resources is often not the biggest hurdle standing between you and your success, but a lack of resourcefulness.

My mission was clear. I needed to devise ways of raising funds for my electronics project under my own steam. I now had a clear objective, desired outcome and a measurable tangible result to focus on. So the game commenced.

> **Startup Pro Insight:** It's interesting to note that once I had clearly identified **WHAT** I needed to do and **WHY**, the mechanics of **HOW** became so much simpler to define and action.

Believe it or not, the story of the young entrepreneurial adventure that I am about to bestow on you here is totally true and based upon the facts as I saw them at the time and recall them now. The only elements added to the story are my narrations which serve to highlight the experiences and insights gained from within the business world since. At the time I had no clue what I was doing (some may say that's still the case!) but I have referenced which business models, methodologies and principles I was unknowingly applying where, when and how.

THE YOUNG ENTREPRENEUR

My grandparent's weekly visits were not only eagerly awaited due to the prospect of an afternoon of extreme confectionery indulgence; there was much more at stake from a young entrepreneur's perspective. In addition to the outstanding selection of what seemed like dinner plate sized cream buns on offer, my generous grandparents also awarded us with three or four tubes of sweets a week. Perhaps this could be considered a little excessive by today's health conscious standards, but this was the 1970s, a time when it was still acceptable to play with lead soldiers, drink from hoses, put sunset yellow colouring in everything, ride bikes and skateboards without helmets and actually engage in regular physical activity. Anyway, back to the story. In the minds of my brother and sister they had a fistful of goodies to be scoffed and glutinously enjoyed at the first opportunity, but in the curious and active mind of the young entrepreneur something else was happening, an opportunity had emerged and a plan was taking shape.

> **Startup Pro Insight:** Whilst most of those around you will be seeing things at face value, the entrepreneur's mind will be avidly at work evaluating any number of scenarios and options for identifying opportunities to maximise the potential returns in any given situation. In a nutshell, the herd will opt for instant gratification vs. the entrepreneur's view of longer-term opportunity, investment and potential return.

Unlike my siblings, who would enjoy the face value gratification of said confectionery windfall, my perspective was very different. In my quickly developing entrepreneurial mind I no longer had sweets to eat, I had something much more valuable. I had raw materials, no, it was far better than that, I had **ASSETS** that could be capitalised upon and turned into revenue and even better, **PROFIT**. The real question though was this. How could I create value with these assets, monetise that value and more importantly translate that value into hard cash? From a now eleven-year old's simplistic perspective the answer was simple. I would open my own sweet shop of course. Perfect, but wait, I had a small issue right there. Who, bearing in mind that this blistering new enterprise would be based in my living room or maybe the hallway, would be my customers or as I call them my *"interested audience"*? By the way, after much deliberation I chose the hallway as the better option because it had more footfall. Then I had the Ah ha, epiphany light bulb moment. If I opened my shop late on Wednesday afternoons my unsuspecting grandparents could become my customers. I know, genius. Not only would my wonderful grandparents deliver the raw ingredients directly to me, which were of course FREE, all I would need to do to generate a whopping great profit would be to add some additional value and sell that value on. This stuff was simple. No, it was more than that; it was easy.

Remember to keep thinking like a child.

Startup Pro Insight: The more value you can add at your stage of the value chain the more profit you can make. The value chain is simply the journey that your product or service takes from creation through to the final sale to the end customer. The most value and consequently profit that can be created happens at the beginning and the end of the value chain. So, if you are creating the product and service idea, producing it and selling it directly to your end customers you have two profitable stages of the value chain to profit from. The stages in the middle are less profitable. Those who distribute and deliver products and services as third parties for example are generally able to add less value and so derive less profit as a result (unless of course you can sell at huge scale). In an ideal world you should look to be the creator and the seller to maximise profits. In my little enterprise the ideal solution would have been to make and sell my sweets directly to my customers. This is a simple concept but one of the most vital because once you know what a product or service value chain looks like you can start to see where adding the most value can deliver the most profit.

So how was I going to create additional value with several tubes of sweets? I had to come up with an attractive proposition which was compelling enough for my customers to part with their money and buy my products. I did not need to reinvent the wheel here and the answer to me was easy. I just asked myself a few simple questions:

What was the problem I was trying to solve?

Did enough people have the problem?

Would those people be willing to pay me if I could solve that problem for them?

How much would they be willing to pay?

Ok, so at the age of eleven I did not know that these were the questions I needed to ask but with years of experience and hindsight I do now. The questions I really asked myself at that point were as follows (and they are still completely valid by the way):

How would I like to buy sweets?

(The problem or desire for my customers)

What would make me want to buy them? (The value proposition)

How much could I charge? (The value of the problem to be solved)

Many **"experts"** may quite rightly tell you that you should not only sell what you like. I have come to call this **"orange jumper syndrome"**: you love orange jumpers and you're a medium in size AND that's exactly what you decide to sell to everyone on the planet regardless of your **"interested audience's"** wants, needs and desires. That's great of course if you have identified an insatiable mass audience who love medium sized orange jumpers. In reality that particular example might be a little too niche to turn into a robust business (though if you love a challenge I'm more than happy to be proven wrong here). I would agree with this way of thinking to a certain degree, but that may be dependent upon how close you are to your target market.

Many small business owners share their ideal customers' profile because they set out to solve a problem that they had in the first place and then discovered that others like them had the same problem. This is arguably the best starting point for any new fledgling startup enterprise.

> **Startup Pro Insight:** If you find one person, group, tribe or business with a problem you're likely to find hundreds if not thousands with exactly the same problem, bottleneck or pain point that needs resolving.

So, back to the story. My friends and I liked sweets but with limited funds we could only buy one or two varieties in packs or opt for a *"pick n mix"* selection, but that was much more expensive and you got less for your money (*The Problem*). My friends and I could have, of course, pooled our financial resources, but with limited interest and the inevitable squabbles that result from such arrangements at that age this was not a viable option. Later on though, I would discover that in the right circumstances this type of deal, known as a *"joint venture"*, could be a highly lucrative method of quickly accelerating traction, income and profits. My unique selling proposition then was simple. I would add value by splitting the packs of sweets down and repackaging them into smaller variety packs (*Adding Value*). That way I could sell them cheaper than a standard *"pick n mix"* selection or an entire tube whilst offering greater variety in smaller affordable quantities (*The Solution*). I would then sell them back to my customers (grandparents) for a whooping profit. What a great model, if only I could figure out how to do that on a massive scale today. Any suggestions drop me a line and we'll do a joint venture and share the profits 50/50, sound fair?

I duly set up my new sweet shop one Wednesday afternoon and unsurprisingly sales were brisk. I say unsurprisingly because to the budding eleven-year-old entrepreneur everything and anything was possible. Negativity, doubts and lack of confidence did not feature in my life at that age. In my young and free adventurous mind all ideas worked like a charm with little or no risk of anything ever going wrong, and besides my wonderful grandparents were not about to spoil the party for me. More on why asking family and friends to validate your ideas is not ideal later.

At the end of the first day's trading I had made a bit of money and still had some sweets leftover. A great result, yes, but more importantly I had quickly validated that my initial idea (hypothesis) had *"legs"*. I had also enquired with my grandparents and parents whether the sweet selection was good enough and whether I should be changing any aspects of my offerings to improve them in any way (I really did this by the way). My customers' feedback (or as I now know it: **The Voice Of The Customer**) was glowing of course, and so it was time to get committed and start thinking about this enterprise a little more seriously.

The following Wednesday afternoon I once again rolled out my makeshift sweet shop and once again sales were brisk. I had indeed uncovered a winning formula. No, it was more than that, in my mind I had a runaway success on my hands, or so I thought. The first couple of weeks had gone down a storm but subsequent weeks saw sales take a significant dip. This unfortunate slip had left me with a surplus of stock, little money and, even more perturbingly, very little in the way of profit. What had gone so wrong? I had after all validated my idea and had even made an early profit. The questions I needed quick answers to were obvious:

What had caused such a rapid dip in demand? And more importantly, what could I do to turn it around?

Startup Pro Insight: It turns out I had made some classic rookie entrepreneur mistakes:

Mistake No 1: I was selling to a very limited number of customers.

Mistake No 2: My product range was also limited.

Mistake No 3: I had no system for leveraging customer engagements to make additional sales.

Mistake No 4: My customers were both **"invested and biased"**. In essence my **"interested audience"** were friends and family.

Mistake No 5: I thought I had a business when in fact what I had on my hands was the **"novelty effect"**. A fad, a flash in the pan that was simply not sustainable in the long-term. Basically, my extremely limited albeit friendly customers had got bored after the initial novelty had worn off.

It had dawned on me that my originally identified customer base was not my real interested audience after all. I not only needed a bigger market, I also needed to identify my real target market. Let me think. Where would an eleven-year-old boy find a sugar mad ravenous *"interested audience"* who had little money but a big appetite for their favourite sweets, packaged up in low-cost ready to go variety packs? That's my avatar or ideal customer profile by the way. The wheels of the young entrepreneur's mind were just starting to gather momentum.

A Cunning Plan

Once again *"happy"* Wednesday (delivery day) had rolled around and the usual free sweetie stocks were duly delivered. Like a hustling drug dealer, I would separate all of the sweets from the tubes and then make up a number of variety packs all containing about eight sweets each, which I duly wrapped into cling film baggies (I told you I was like a hustling drug dealer). My immediate problem was that I really did not have enough stock to make the financial impact I needed. My solution was **OPR** *or* **Other People's Resources**. In my case that meant my brother and sister's resources. I made a deal to take their sweets and pay them an ongoing share of the profits in return for their initial investment. Now I had investors, which for reference is both a curse and a blessing, but more on that later.

> **Startup Pro Insight:** Whilst many businesses leverage **OPM (Other People's Money)** to finance their new enterprises (a topic I discuss in detail later) **OPR** or Other People's Resources should not be underestimated or undervalued as a valuable area of alternative capital you can leverage. Cash investment for a new startup in the early days can appear high-risk and therefore a much harder sell than negotiating the use, loan or access to resources that others already have. Think about this from your own perspective. Would you be more open to lending a hand, providing some expertise, time and effort on a project or stumping up a cold hard cash investment? I use OPR regularly and in some cases it's actually a far more valuable asset than just

money. Money is a commodity that's available everywhere. Specialist knowledge, experience, expertise, time and effort however are far scarcer.

My cunning plan was simple. I would take my little variety sweet packs directly to my hot target audience (school friends) and sell them. I figured that I had a hot product and an ***"interested audience"*** that I could satisfy, and at scale. This met my requirements on a number of levels.

1) I knew that I could sell my product at an attractive price and still make a risk-free profit, albeit because I had not actually paid for the stock in the first place as my grandparents had unknowingly become my stealth investors. Investors may be the wrong word here as they never saw a penny profit, but hey. Tick.

2) A mixed variety bag would be appealing to my customers (school friends) as they got a little bit of everything rather than buying one single product, and at a "perceived" cheaper price. Tick.

3) I had identified a clear gap in the market with little competition for my value offering. Tick.

My initial rollout was, in essence, an experiment to test my original ideas and assumptions about my audience and my perception of their problem. I needed to validate that my solution would solve that problem and was valuable enough from my customers' perspective for them to buy.

Once the first day of trading at school was over I took the money home and counted it out. I then counted it out again and again and again. Why the numerous recounts you may ask? Well simply because, and this sounds silly all these years later, I thought I had miscounted. As an eleven-year-old with extremely limited fiscal resources I really could not believe how much profit I had made in one day from my simple little idea. I was now sold hook, line and sinker on this entrepreneurial lark. I saved my first entrepreneurial winnings, paid my brother and sister their profit share and waited with baited breath for the following week's delivery of raw materials to be delivered by my stealth investors (grandparents). By the way my brother and sister were now also sold on the prospect of continued profits. Well, they were once I pointed out that they could go and buy their own sweets with some of the profit and still have cash leftover, or they could choose to reinvest into my little expansion program.

In the meantime, a portion of the profits I was making each week were being reinvested back into my little enterprise whilst some were funding my electronics project as per the original requirement for fund raising. I had now gained a position of sufficiency where I was making regular revenue, producing a profit and tentatively investing in future projects.

> **Startup Pro Insight:** You may remember that I mentioned my electronic robot building project at the beginning of the book and how I needed to raise funds for the electrical components needed to build it. Based upon my early **"sweet shop"** successes I used the knowledge gained to

also turn this little side project into another little entrepreneurial money-spinner.

After due consideration I thought that I could build the robots on mass and sell them for a decent profit. I could even get some of my geekier electronics friends to help me build them in a production line setup at weekends. Once again, I tested my ideas early and in doing so immediately exposed a critical flaw in my plan. The trouble with my initial approach was that robots built by hand from component parts took time to build and, as I had discovered as part of my dummy run, lots of it. I had to come up with a financially viable alternative. My profitable alternative was to pivot slightly on my original idea.

I had already highlighted that the lengthiest and subsequently most expensive stage in the **"value chain"** was the actual build stage. Unfortunately, I had absolutely no way of outsourcing or automating this process nearly enough to make it economically viable, so I came up with the idea of removing the build process altogether.

Why not farm out the most lengthy and costly elements of the robots' production (the assembly and build) to my customers? My target market after all had a huge hobbyist interest in electronics, gizmos and putting together projects. I did some simple calculations and quickly discovered that it was much more profitable to draw up some basic assembly plans which could be easily photocopied and supplied with the electronic component parts needed to produce a simple DIY robot kit for avid techie fans. I later discovered that I had additional markets I hadn't even thought of including radio control model fans and general modellers. I had unknowingly stumbled across a great business model where I could develop the product once, easily source and package low-cost parts and charge a premium for adding and delivering perceived high value. What's more I only had to do the development once and in doing so would largely extract myself from heavy ongoing commitment. All I needed to do was to make up the DIY kit boxes and mail them out. This left me with ample time to focus on other opportunities and products and even extend the range of robot model offerings. I ran a couple of small, cheap classified ads (I used some sweet shop profit for this) in electronics hobbyist magazines (remember this was in the days before the Internet). I went on to make a decent profit on this little enterprise for about eighteen months before a large commercial retailer went and did exactly the same thing. (I also learned a lot about knowing when an opportunity has run its course and when it's time to move on, but more on that little gem of a topic later).

Can you start seeing how simple ideas start to grow and present a myriad of opportunities that would have been missed if you had not got started in the first place? (Hint – that happens a lot in the world of the entrepreneur)

Anyway, back to my little sweet shop enterprise. By this time, I had a little routine of acquiring stock, splitting packs and re packing them (**adding value**) and selling. I repeated this routine over and over, in fact it was now much more than a routine, I had developed the entire process into a simple standardised process that continued to produce a healthy return on investment every single week (more on the value of developing standardised processes and systems later). To be honest, my profits were never going to be anything less than healthy considering that I had absolutely zero overheads and free raw materials at this point. If I could not make a profit with this setup I might as well pack up my entrepreneurial bags and call it a day.

> **Startup Pro Insight:** - By this time the penny had finally dropped. I had developed a simple little business by identifying an opportunity and fulfilling a need. Most importantly though, I had acted upon it. I would later discover that the **"acting upon it"** part was a common Achilles' heel that stops many wannabe entrepreneurs in their tracks.

> **Startup Pro Insight:** Here is a QSS (Quick, Small & Simple) micro startup framework model for building high income products and services. Note: this method will not apply to all opportunities but the more of these guiding principles you can apply to your own products and services the more income and profits you will generate whilst minimising the amount of effort and time investment required.

Simple, easy and quick to produce.

Adds tangible value.

Has high demand.

Is highly consumable.

Has repeat business potential (repeat sales, upselling, cross selling, down selling).

Can be easily scaled.

Premium prices can be charged.

Can be automated as much as possible via processes and systems (removing your time and effort involvement and in doing so leverages passivity).

If you have a cost-effective consumable product that your customers will purchase on an ongoing basis (think repeatable models like subscriptions here) with a way of adding value to enhance the offer, at a price that customers are willing to pay you a premium for you will have a great business model. Integrate that with a captive market (more on the advantages of a captive market later, as well as the downsides which my enterprise ultimately became a victim of) and you will be onto a sure-fire winning formula.

One of my primary unique selling points was that my customers had easy access to me and did not have to queue at the school's *"tuck shop"* or pay their expensive prices for limited choice. By this point though I had a growing problem. It was a great problem to have, but a problem nonetheless. I had a situation where I now had more customers and demand than products to sell, which in turn led to two things happening. One good and one bad.

> **The good** - Due to growing demand and the fact I had a somewhat captive audience I was able to raise my prices slightly. I had more demand than supply (scarcity) which allowed me to maximise my prices and subsequently my profits.

> **The bad** – Whilst scarcity can drive prices up, there is a tipping point where this becomes unsustainable and given that my target market had limited funds I could only maximise my returns so far before my customers would top out and be forced back into the arms of the competition, in this case the school tuck shop. In my situation with my model, scarcity was not the way to go. I needed to leverage my position and service that captive audience at scale. My main challenge at that point was that I really had to solve the limited stock problem, and yes, for those of you already ahead of the game, I might actually have to start paying for stock. Good job I did not have any shareholders other than my brother and sister to keep happy.

I was in no doubt that my growing business operation could not be sustained in the long-term based upon my grandparents' weekly *"investment"*, even though they were now supporting my little enterprise by providing me with a ton of extra sweets a week. It was no good, I would have to start buying my own stock. I started to make purchases from a local sweet shop and almost immediately exposed several additional benefits and potential opportunities.

> **Startup Pro Insight:** Opportunities have a habit of starting to gather momentum when you start doing stuff. **I quickly discovered that opportunities are actually the outcomes and consequences of action and effort.** You will notice that few opportunities present themselves of their own fruition. History proves that the most innovative products, groundbreaking discoveries and game changing inventions only happened as a direct result of someone somewhere doing something, and often doing it wrongly and getting very different outcomes and results from those expected.

As I mentioned, changing my supply chain and going to a shop to purchase my stock presented me with several previously unseen advantages. I now had the benefit of larger product ranges to choose from which increased my capacity to expand my variety packs and produce a different range of offerings. The change also gave me the capability to provide a number of options based upon different customer types and buying propensities. I would learn much later that this was called customer segmentation. The most important discovery however was that the additional product choice meant I could also introduce a customised *"to order" service* that would attract a premium price and generate more profit for no additional effort or cost on my part.

These small but effective evolutions did however introduce yet another challenge for my budding business. Due to the growing popularity of my little venture the queue at break times was getting bigger and bigger, but service was getting slower and slower. This problem had developed not because my prices were cheaper, in fact by this time I was charging a slight premium for my offerings. The growing demand was because my product was not available at the tuck shop (*uniqueness*). I was selling exactly what my customers wanted and were requesting. I had unknowingly discovered a simple way of accelerating my sales and profit (*The Voice Of The Customer*).

> **Startup Pro Insight:** Taking the simple step of gaining feedback from my customers gave me the unique insights I needed to provide them with exactly what they wanted whilst maximising my own revenue and profits. The perfect win-win combination.

> **Startup Pro Insight:** My growing success in the field of confectionery fulfilment was now having the detrimental effect of diluting one of my most valuable Unique Selling Points (USPs): my speed of service. I had to resolve this challenge and quickly. The most obvious way to do this was to get some of my friends to take my sweets and start selling them at different locations around the school on my behalf. I did not have the budget, experience or margin to take them on and pay them utilising a traditional employment salary model, but I could and would willingly pay them a commission on all products sold. I even included a volume sales commission structure. Again, another opportunity

presented itself here that would have the net result of minimising the cost of my sales team. On many occasions my hungry **"sales team"** would take **"commission"** payments in sweet packs or sometimes a mix of sweets and money, but more often than not in sweets alone. This was a win-win situation and I will tell you why. Firstly, I would give them a generous discount price so they would get more sweets than they could buy with their money. Secondly, and more importantly, this was a great deal for me as the cost price of the discounted sweets **"paid"** to them was much less than the real monetary value of paying them hard cash.

Startup Pro Insight: When you break it down, becoming a successful entrepreneur appeared to be based upon becoming proficient in just four key areas:

Identifying opportunities and acting on them (The Problem).

Developing solutions to resolve problems, remove bottlenecks, relieve pain points and fulfil emotional desires.

Delivering value - Helping others to get what they want.

Getting paid - Defining exactly how to receive adequate remuneration.

By the way, at this point I was now unknowingly scaling my operation.

As I progressed I encountered yet another entrepreneurial challenge. My latest little spanner in the works was that I was attracting far too much attention from my competition, or in my case the school tuck shop and senior teaching staff. To combat this little inconvenience and to ensure that I could still manage to continue with my expanding enterprise I gave a quantity of my sweet packs (which incidentally had become a full-time after school packaging job) to some of my friends who would go off to other areas around the school and sell on my behalf for a commission. Although I did not know it at the time, I had effectively franchised my operation with independent vendors selling my products for me by leveraging my established brand and reputation. I later cottoned on to the fact that they should have been paying me for the privilege rather than me paying them a straight commission, but hey you learn something new every day. I now understand that I was inadvertently scaling my operation. More sales people meant more sales, which in turn meant increased revenue growth and profits.

With sales on the rise, the next natural move was to start negotiating better deals from my suppliers. By this time I was going to a number of sweet shops to both mitigate potential supply issues and introduce some competition for supply based upon the growing size of my purchases (**volume**). I was now buying sweets by the box load. I did manage to negotiate the prices to a degree but was largely unsuccessful due to my complete lack of negotiation skills, knowledge and experience in this area at that time. What I really needed to start doing was looking for ways to cut out the retailing middleman altogether and start buying the sweets from a more direct source. In my case that would mean going directly to a wholesaler, which was successfully navigated when an older friend's brother (thank you Martin) went to the local cash and carry to buy stock on my behalf, for a small percentage of course. This entrepreneurial mindset, as it turns out, appears to be everywhere.

I realised much later, and with a little experience and hindsight, that I had in fact successfully navigated the complex world of the startup. I had intuitively built myself a little business from the ground up based upon nothing more than the burning necessity to do so. I had never read a business book, I didn't even know they existed, and to be honest I would not have done anything differently if I had. This experience taught me a lot about starting, running and scaling a small startup enterprise and as I would later discover this process could be distilled down into a simple repeatable system that could be applied over and over again whilst significantly flattening the steep learning curve.

I was riding high on the success of my thriving operation. I had money in my pocket and a seemingly Midas touch when it came to maximising the resources I had. What I was blissfully unaware of at the time however were the downsides, those unforeseen and often ignored risks that you never see coming until it's too late. At some point in your budding entrepreneurial career you will get to experience an unexpected downturn, or even worse a catastrophic downfall. If you don't get to experience either at some point then you're either a unicorn case or probably weren't doing enough in the first place. My awakening to the downsides of walking the entrepreneurial path was well and truly in the post. I never saw it coming and it abruptly ended my little enterprise literally overnight.

Startup Pro Insight: You cannot plan for the inevitable failures that **WILL** occur. I say inevitable because being an entrepreneur is all about the inevitability of failure, interruption and challenges. All of these scenarios will happen at some point to some degree during your entrepreneurial career. Nothing lasts forever even if you're riding the heady wave of success right now, eventually it will fizzle out and die. Let me give you a simple real-world piece of advice from the trenches here. Like the Grim Reaper you cannot avoid failure, in fact it's a necessary part of your entrepreneurial evolution, a rite of passage if you like. In the same way that exercise resistance builds muscle and makes you stronger, so the resistance that challenges and failure creates also builds strength, increases your resolve and drives future successes. The truth is I have had more failures than successes, it's just that the successes have completely outshone the failures. I would never have had the highs of success had I not experienced the lows of failure and had the opportunity to learn the valuable lessons, and rules of the game, along the way.

THE MIGHTY FALL

And They All Do - Eventually

My little *"on the side"* business enterprise continued to go from strength to strength, I was Mr. Big, the confectionery king, *"Mr. Tuck"* or *"The Friar"* as I had become affectionately known. I was numero-uno and thought I was untouchable but eventually, as is the case with most things in life, nothing lasts forever. Tongues started to wag, rumours began to rumble and well to cut a long story short I was, as they say in schoolboy parlance, well and truly *"grassed up"*. As a result of this unplanned and unwanted broadcast my little moonlighting confectionery business secret was out, and the school's head wasted no time in bringing my little flurry into the world of entrepreneurialism to an unceremonious and quite abrupt end. This particular party was well and truly over.

> **Startup Pro Insight:** The thing about endings, as with beginnings, is that they often happen very quickly.

You will never see the lightning strike that hits you and you can never plan for avoiding it completely if you play out in stormy weather. All you can do is build the capability to roll with the punches and have mechanisms in place to deal with the outcomes and associated fallout as effectively, positively and proactively as possible. Most of all though you will need to be able to develop the ability and resilience to move on when it's time. I can't stress the importance of those two points enough. Far too many people get caught up in the emotional side of a perceived failure and windup making bad decisions because of it. My advice here, keep the facts straight and ban emotions to the bench.

ASHES & THE PHOENIX

Although down I was by no means out, and like any good entrepreneur I was quick to regroup, take stock, examine the options and readjust my plans, after all I had everything in place to continue. I still had an operation, a willing team that wanted to earn money and a system for running it. What I no longer had were customers by the bucket load, and captive ones at that.

> **Startup Pro Insight:** Whilst I still had eager customers, my access to them had been thwarted. That's an important point to take on board. Simply identifying a market does not necessarily mean that you can access, penetrate, leverage or profit from it directly. Sometimes you need help to do it and that's what partnerships and joint ventures are for.

What I needed to do now was to identify and cultivate a new customer base. I still had the regulars who I could sell to, but my large captive audience were for all intents and purposes off-limits. With a joint venture deal with the school *"tuck shop"* very much off the cards I was driven inconveniently underground somewhat by my school's short-sightedness to encourage and develop my entrepreneurial skills. I needed to quickly develop new markets or new ways to leverage the old one.

> **Startup Pro Insight:** As you'll hear more about later, an unexpected opportunity had presented itself as a result of my operations demise. Even in seemingly bad times there is

always a rough diamond waiting to be polished and sold on for a profit.

The obvious and only choice to me now was to concentrate my efforts on the most significant and important problem, which was developing a target audience outside the control and jurisdiction of teaching staff and school management. This was the route I took but it was not as easy or as simple as I had first assumed.

Once again, I got the opportunity to learn first-hand a couple of invaluable business lessons from the front line. The first of which was that being within the confines of the school gates I had the extreme luxury of having what I now know to have been a captive audience. I had vastly underestimated the value of this at the time but know very differently now.

I had competition in the shape of the *"tuck shop"* but it was limited, and the available market and audience could not go anywhere else. Outside of the school gates however I not only had to cope with a whole heap of unwanted competition, but most of the school's young inhabitants were not allowed to venture off site at break times and after school they either went straight home having run out of money or spent it at one of my numerous competitors because they had more choice to do so. I had lost the key advantage of a captive audience. Although I was eager to continue my venture I had the good sense and instinct to know when to call it a day and move on to new opportunities, and after a couple of months of fruitless effort that's exactly what I did.

Startup Pro Insight: knowing when an opportunity has run its course is an art. It's often emotionally difficult to do, but heavily investing your most precious resources in hard work that returns little is a waste. Learn to be objective and focus your resources and efforts on new opportunities that can produce easier results. In short, don't keep pumping when the well has run dry. Go dig a new well.

I have learned the hard way that most of us entrepreneurs are way too emotional when it comes to our ideas, projects and businesses. Whilst it's emotion that drives us to act, gives us our intuition and motivates us, those same emotions can work against us by making us stick with something that is long dead or is quickly reaching the end of its effective life. It's far more productive and rewarding to start a new chapter by investing your time, money and effort in more fruitful opportunities, and it was that time for me.

As I mentioned in the *"The Mighty Fall"* chapter, my entrepreneurial downfall did present me with an unexpected opportunity. That opportunity was to go and share my entrepreneurial experiences including my business model, difficulties and financial details to various economics classes around the borough's schools. I found this highly entertaining to say the least, because those running the classes were stereotypical economics teachers who had no real-world experience of putting the textbook theories they were teaching into practice. I, on the other hand, had done it from scratch at just twelve years of age. I did not get paid for those talks, presentations and knowledge share sessions, but once again I know differently today.

Many of you reading this may be wondering how sharing my experiences to others for free was such a great opportunity? The answer is really simple. It gave me the chance to get up and speak in public. It's where I quickly honed my early speaking and presenting skills. It was also where I discovered that I had a natural talent for imparting my knowledge, experience and expertise to others effectively. Skills which have paid significant dividends ever since.

> **Startup Pro Insight:** Opportunities are often not immediate and have to be banked, cultivated and developed over time for later use. A lot of your future success will depend upon turning your experiences, knowledge and expertise into "success" cultivating building blocks for use at a later date.

My early entrepreneurial experiences were a great learning opportunity for me, even if most of them were completely ad-hoc and naturally organic. The thing was, my actions were born out of pure necessity and based upon nothing more than my own ability to apply a common sense approach and simple problem solving skills to get the job done. This early endeavour into the entrepreneurial world went on to pave the way for a range of other hair-brained (my Dad's words, not mine) schemes including fireworks made from water (ok I know that sounds mad, but I was working on the basis that hydrogen was a key element of H2O), cake making, bicycle repair services, gardening, bottle collecting and home delivery shopping services (by bike). The standout commonality here is that the principles I used, albeit completely unknowingly at the time, were the same principles applied within just about every single startup business on the planet, irrespective of size, type, industry and market.

Startup Pro Insight: Some businesses work out and some don't. I have had more failures than successes and so will you. That's why it's so critical to get started quickly and discover what works, what doesn't and more importantly why, before you invest too much valuable time, money and effort. Do a dummy run, test and validate with paying customers that you have a real opportunity before making any serious commitment, not the other way around.

The Inevitability Of Change

Much of what you may have been told about startups is untrue.

We all know that the world is changing at breakneck speed and that the old ways of working are dead, yet many still persist in trying to use the old, outdated and ineffective systems, methods and thinking to make progress. This is no more evident than in the flourishing world of the entrepreneur. Like everything else today, setting up and running a business has inextricably changed. Availability of cheap accessible technology has allowed truly global markets to be quite literally on your doorstep. And the best bit? It's cheap and easy, and I mean really cheap and easy, to get started.

Today's startup winners quickly learn this new game. They proactively embrace technology and change. They take control and fully accept responsibility and accountability for what they do and put themselves firmly in the driving seat of their own destinies and successes. Never before has it been so easy to get started and launch a startup. I know of several global businesses that have been quite literally started from the kitchen table with less than one thousand dollars. Many of these bootstrapped startups have gone on to become large businesses with multi-million dollar turnovers. That kind of shift and evolution in the marketplace means just one thing:

That it's just as easy for you to join them.

Tomorrow's successful entrepreneurs are those who recognise their worth and value and can package their knowledge, experiences, and expertise into products, services and tools that add huge value to customers by solving their most challenging problems, easing pain points, removing bottlenecks or massaging emotional feelings and desires. By the way, no one buys anything that is not meeting at least one of those four crucial elements.

> **Startup Pro Insight:** There is a direct correlation between the size of a problem to be solved and the size of the reward and remuneration. Far too many new entrepreneurs underestimate and undervalue what they know and in doing so leave money and opportunity on the table.

Most new startups nowadays are completely self-funded or, as we like to call them, *"bootstrapped"* businesses. Many owners launch their startups and work on them part-time until the revenue generated meets or exceeds their current income levels or just generates the extra income desired.

I know a growing number of *"on the side"* micro startup entrepreneurs who generate an additional $1-3,000.00 per month on a part-time basis. They are happy to continue working the business part-time on the side and use the profits to fund luxury purchases including new cars, holidays or a house move. Others have quickly built businesses that have far exceeded their traditional employment incomes. Some have even developed their *"on the side"* portfolio of business enterprises into *multiple six and in some extreme cases seven figure* annual incomes, all whilst giving them back their most valuable assets; *freedom, choice and, most importantly, discretionary time.*

Startups mean different things to different people. Some are started as a labour of love, whilst others are built completely by accident whilst trying to solve a specific problem for themselves only to discover that many others had the same or similar problems that needed resolving. Some entrepreneurs build businesses with a clear vision of being acquired in the future, while others have made a conscious decision to develop small, simple boutique lifestyle businesses that provide a comfortable income with no desire to grow the business beyond that.

Defining your end game in great detail early on is often not immediately critical, but the more defined you can be in terms of your long-term "vision" and roadmap, the easier it will be to develop and execute the strategies needed to deliver the desired outcome.

> **Startup Pro Insight:** Paying customers, now that's a business. Anything else is called a hobby.

Why, Why & Why?

People launch startups for a number of reasons but often it's out of sheer necessity. I have lost count of the number of highly skilled professionals I know who have been made redundant and could not gain another traditional employment position. Others have had an epiphany moment that clears the mist and provides complete clarity where upon they suddenly realise that their destiny, lives and freedom have all been dictated to and controlled by others who can, and so often do, freely change everything on a whim.

It's a common misconception that entrepreneurialism and self-employment is a high-risk proposition and that employment is the more stable secure route (**think about who told you that by the way**). Now whilst I will admit that **"going it alone"** can be challenging from time to time, I would argue that relying upon employment as your sole source of income is in fact a far riskier proposition in that you have little or no control over anything.

I would much rather have some level of accepted uncertainty and risk that I'm able to control, negate and balance as required rather than unpredictable uncertainty I can't. Ultimately becoming a full-time or part-time startup pro is about making the decision to be responsible and accountable for standing on your own two feet and making your own way in the world. If you're not making your own plans you're part of someone else's, and for me that just does not sit well.

Getting Started

Ok so you love the idea of being an *"on the side"* micro startup entrepreneur, the life, the money, and the freedom? Well I have some bad news for you and you are not going to like it because I'm afraid it applies to 95% (or perhaps even more) of you reading this book right now. I'm not going to dress this up and I make no apologies for being so blunt and abrupt. The majority of you reading this book are wasting your time and will fail to produce anything lasting or meaningful, and here's why.

Almost every single one of you will waste a large proportion of your most valuable assets (time, money and effort) on the three **'P's; Planning, Perfectionism, and Procrastination,** rather than **taking action**. You will become obsessed with and focused on what you think needs to be done in future, striving for perfection or procrastinating over too many choices, rather than just focusing on and delivering the results that matter. Let's take a quick look at each of the three 'P's in a little more detail so you can recognise the warning signs and behaviours that create undesirable outcomes.

Planning

Whilst some planning is good for setting core strategies, basic direction and timelines, doing too much of it does have a considerable detrimental downside. The problem with planning is that it's mostly guesswork, based upon no more than assumptions, hypotheses and uncertainty. Most who strive to launch their own startups end up stuck in a constant cycle of non-productive *"action planning"*, a kind of proactive procrastination if you like. The end result being that they never launch anything of real substance. Yes you may have hundreds of great award winning *"millionaire"* or even *"billionaire"* ideas in your back pocket, yes you may plan loads of stuff and yes you may have filled your time with *"busy work"*, but let me ask you a simple qualifying question:

How many profit generating revenue streams will you be able to hold your hands up to in three, six or even twelve months' time? Unless you can control planning and focus on action and execution my bet is not many.

Perfectionism

Getting stuck in a never-ending spiral of perfectionism is one of the most common afflictions facing new entrepreneurs. Many mistakenly believe perfectionism to be a good thing and a condition to be continually worked towards. Whilst striving to deliver your best is of course an admirable quality, it's also important to keep in mind that perfectionism is often subconsciously used to emotionally disguise delaying tactics. Perfectionists are often perceived as high performers when in fact the very opposite is true, with many lacking self-confidence, having feelings of overwhelm, doubt, insecurity and a wanting to avoid failure at all costs, which of course they can't. Perfectionists are rarely prolific performers because they expend so much time and effort seeking *"perceived"* perfection that delivery is often conspicuous by its absence. How many great artists, award winning actors, writers, musicians and business people do you think exist in the world right now? Tens of thousands, hundreds of thousands, millions? We will never know because their work will remain hidden from the world in a constant state of *"rework and improvement"*. Don't make the mistake of thinking that perfection equals performance. In the real world that's almost never the case.

Procrastination

Just as perfectionism can be an emotional way of putting a respectful spin on delaying tactics, so procrastination can also be an emotional disguise for a lack of interest, motivation, purpose and commitment. No matter how much you may idealise the *"the end result"*, if your heart and soul are not in it, procrastination will take hold every time. In essence procrastination is simply a cognitive response or story that we tell ourselves to justify our inaction and lack of progress. Procrastinators will often find themselves overwhelmed with choice, get stuck in ruts and generally lack organisation, purpose and direction. This is why identifying your true purpose is so critical. Those with a true love and passion for what they do rarely cite procrastination as a hindrance to productivity or performance. If you find yourself constantly procrastinating it might be wise to take a good hard look at what you are doing, and why it matters. It could of course be that you have drifted a little over time and just need to realign to what's important for you. A quick re-evaluation of your purpose and mission will quickly see you back on track focusing on objectives, outcomes and results that really matter. Procrastinating is not all bad news though. Recent scientific research has shown that mindful procrastination can be extremely valuable in the fields of decision making, idea creation and solving complex problems. Like everything, balance is the key.

Part II

Startup Strategies, Lessons & Insights

Please note: The strategies and insights I have focused on within this book are certainly not intended to be exhaustive but more of a starting point to get you thinking, acting and performing like a startup pro. I also want you to be able define and focus on the most important things that you really need to get done to get something up and running quickly and, most importantly of all, producing value for your customers and income for you.

1

WHAT'S YOUR FREEDOM?

Freedom is very subjective. Your version of freedom, choices and goals will be specific to you and will likely be very different from my own. Your passions, motivations and drivers will ultimately be your guide on what you do, how you do it and why. Some of you reading this will want to ditch full-time employment completely and do what you love and get paid for it. Others may be forced into action due to changes in personal and or professional circumstances that are beyond your control. Some like myself simply love the mechanics and work involved in building out new ventures, alongside the advantages of accelerating their capability to make their own decisions. For some that may mean early retirement, working part-time or becoming more financially secure, knowing that they have multiple sources of dependable income should the worst happen.

Although freedom and choice mean different things to different people, one thing I can tell you for sure is this: you absolutely need to be crystal clear about what your version of freedom looks like before you start. It can change along the way of course, and more than likely will, but you need to know what that looks like for you right now. In short, you need to be clear on the following:

Your Motivation(s) - Why are you doing what you are doing, what is your purpose?

Your Outcomes(s) - What does your future state look like?

Your Objective(s) - What needs to be true in order to deliver the desired state?

Your Result(s) - What are the measurable benefits delivered once completed?

These points not only dictate the *what*, *why*, *how* and *when* of the project, they also define a simple framework for setting a clear strategic roadmap, identifying measurable progress and formulating the success criteria that will indicate when you have achieved your desired goals.

2

You're a Scientist

Just in case you are one of the statistical 50% of people who never finish a book I'm going to get one of the most important startup pro insight out of the way early on, and here it is:

The Mistake

The most common mistake made by virtually every single new startup entrepreneur is that they invest time, money and effort in STARTING A BUSINESS. *"But wait"* I hear you cry, isn't that exactly what startup entrepreneurs are supposed to do? Else what's the point? Well the answer to that question is, it depends. And it depends on timing. The thing is, new entrepreneurs tend to jump the gun and miss out a fundamental component of the startup process by putting their **"business building"** hats on before they really know what they need to build. Let me explain that in a little more detail. Investing time, effort and often money and starting a business is not the first stage of the process, in fact **"building the business"** comes way down the line.

So if you don't start and build a business upfront, what do you do?

The Solution

The most successful entrepreneurs don't blindly build businesses straight out of the gate, they build labs and carry out experiments. In fact they utilise the same considered methodical approach as a scientist would. Just like a scientist your role first and foremost is to generate new ideas and then design and carry out a number of experiments within controlled environments in order to derive measurable data and insights that can be used to provide evidence of validity. Once your hypothetical business idea has been tested and validated, then and only then should you move onto the development and build phase. By using this simple qualification method many entrepreneurial scientists quickly discover that their original thinking, ideas and assumptions were fundamentally flawed in some way and need to be reworked, re-evaluated or in some cases completely redesigned. The good news about using a scientific *"ring fenced"* testing approach is that it's quick, simple and cheap to do it, and once completed provides very clear insights on the validity of your proposal.

> **Startup Pro Insight:** In order to be successful at anything you need to develop a repeatable and predictable process for identifying opportunities, validating them and then delivering equitable value that you can get paid for.

3

YOU DON'T NEED A YES

"It's far easier to seek forgiveness than approval"

I learned two valuable lessons early on in my life and both have served me well in the years since.

If you wait for others to give you approval before you do anything you have instantly given away your controlling advantage (and yes, it's all about advantage) to someone else. In doing so you have lost the power to make decisions for yourself, and I don't have to tell you how damaging, limiting and disastrous this can be.

If you give someone the opportunity to say *"No"*, guess what they will most likely say? Once you have asked for permission and given away your controlling advantage it's then difficult to go ahead and do it anyway or at least without some unwanted consequences. Don't believe me? Go and seek approval from a member of the middle management team to do something (I pick on middle managers because they can normally only ever say no. Harsh I know but unfortunately true.) When you get the expected *"NO"*, go and do it anyway and watch the inevitable fallout (by the way I cannot be held responsible for any detrimental consequences). Conversely, if you just go and do something without seeking permission the worst that will normally happen in retrospect will be that you may have to explain yourself and possibly get a reprimand of some description. Keep in mind that it's difficult to seriously reprimand proactive thinkers, self-starters and action takers. Whereas doing something after a specific *"no"* has been given is challenging the very authority that stereotypical management types crave, love and think they have, and that, I'm afraid, never ends well.

Just going off and doing stuff is what drives the true entrepreneur. Those qualities are part of our makeup, it's in our DNA. Entrepreneurs are self-starting innovators, people of action and individuals with a bias for curiosity and getting stuff done. They want to see results and as such are more than happy to deal with the consequences later. Remember any outcome to the bustling entrepreneur, good, bad or ugly, is a valuable insight in some way.

Seeking authority and approval will only ever end up with you doing what others want and think can be achieved. Most of the time these limiting attitudes will be used to keep you in your place. Cynical? Perhaps, but based totally upon experience and as I always say:

I can only ever tell you what I know.

4

Learn Once, Apply Many

Now the word *'startup'* has become almost completely synonymous with businesses, and whilst many of the principles, lessons and strategies that I discuss in this book do indeed apply to business startup scenarios, this is just one small area of application. Startup strategies and tools are in fact business agnostic, completely portable and, more importantly, can be easily transferred and implemented across a diverse range of scenarios, including:

Business startups

Launching new departments

Designing new software

Building new products and services

Increasing the success of project delivery

Health

Wealth

Personal growth

Professional development

Everything has to start somewhere, but the most important aspect is developing the capability to gain enough momentum and traction to keep that startup ball in the air and rolling long enough to deliver value to your customers and profit to you. There are many facets to successfully starting and launching a new venture but in the end a startup of any kind does one single thing. It solves problems or, more simply put, it tangibly improves your customers' condition. Becoming a startup pro is not only a highly valued skill to acquire for building and launching successful enterprises, it's a really valuable skill that can be transferred and leveraged within any marketplace. Look at it this way. Nothing happens if your company, or the company or client you work for, can't or won't get started. Learning and defining how the startup process works can often be the springboard from which so many other successes originate. This is one of the most common areas where businesses can falter and stall rather than blossom and progress.

> **Startup Pro Insight:** Remember, above all else, that execution is everything. Organisations are historically poor at execution. Mastering this skill alone and helping others to successfully meet their objectives could be your gateway to a fortune.

5

Concept To Cash

Many startups these days adopt an agile bootstrap approach. That's to say they are small or solo boutique enterprises run and funded solely by the owner(s). As a bootstrap startup owner you will be required to wear many different hats and master many differing skills, including idea generation, sales, marketing, finance, product development, support, IT and logistics. No matter what business you decide to go into there is one simple overarching principle you can use to keep you honest throughout the startup process and it's the *concept to cash principle.* This popular concept penned by technology guru Mary Poppendieck can be applied as the mandatory yardstick for your new venture. What it means is:

> Define the quickest path from your initial conceptual idea through to having paying customers.

The phases and timeline to value delivery should be as short as possible. As we will discuss later, your initial value proposition is not supposed to be the *"all singing, all dancing"* fully functional version of your product or service. Your purpose early on is to develop a test model, or a Minimum Viable Product (MVP) as it is more commonly known, that you can get customers using. This enables you to quickly prove value, reduce assumptions and uncertainty whilst testing the validity of your solution from your customers' perspective. This is the approach agile startups use to gain momentum, traction and revenue so quickly. Remember, become a scientist first; experiment, gather data and validate your ideas before seriously committing and investing your time, money and effort.

Agile startup methodologies are very popular, dare I say it fashionable at the moment, but they are a robust proven method for getting started and delivering customer value quickly. Where possible try and adopt this simple strategy into the very fabric of any new venture that you embark on. Remember, anything that reduces risk, complexity and uncertainty is a valuable asset, especially in the initial early stages.

6

LEARN THE RULES OF THE GAME

It's So Much Easier

Like any game, system or process, there are a number of ways to make it simpler and far less complex. One way to do this is to follow the rules. Shock, horror, follow the rules, "us entrepreneurs make and break them, we don't follow them" I hear you cry. Well stick with me on this one and I will explain. When I say follow the rules, I don't mean that you have to prescriptively follow the rules or that it's in any way mandatory to do so. What I am saying is you should be leveraging the experiences and learnings of others who have already trodden the same path that you are looking to take.

Most people have a general disdain for rules, thinking them to be restrictive, controlling and inflexible, when in fact rules and guidelines are put in place to assist with reaching a successful outcome. Think of rules as guidance, organisation, and governance around any given process or task. Whilst you certainly don't have to follow them, and many don't and decide instead to make up their own rules and discover better more efficient ways of doing things, there is normally a fairly steep learning curve for doing so. In order to provide some clarity around the key differences between rules and guidelines let's take a look at the dictionary meanings of each of the two words:

Rules: "A set of explicit or understood regulations or principles governing conduct or procedure within a particular area of activity."

Guidelines: "General rules, principles, or pieces of advice."

So, in summary: Rules apply a stricter adherence to ensure governance and compliance to specific areas of activity. Guidelines on the other hand are looser more generalised advisories around any given subject matter. Guidelines are not so much written as observed. Trying to circumnavigate any part of a complex system or process usually results in unexpected or detrimental outcomes, and the startup process is no different from any other. Knowing and understanding the rules and guidelines is one thing but following them is something else entirely. Knowing what you should do and then not doing it and you'll only have yourself to blame when it all goes wrong. In the entrepreneurial world this normally gets translated as everything taking twice as long and costing twice as much whilst delivering half the value.

Why would you ever want to make anything harder than it needs to be?

The answer to that question is because we are all fundamentally flawed. Hey, what a surprise. It's a psychological fact that we can't help ourselves when it comes to overcomplicating things and ignoring the good advice that comes from those who are wiser and more experienced than we are. We have a tendency of paying far too much attention to that little demon inside us that proclaims *"I know best"*. You know the one I mean. So why is that? The answer to that question becomes obvious when you understand how we think and cognitively process and develop solutions to problems. As it turns out when faced with a problem to be solved we automatically feel the overwhelming compulsion to contribute. We do this by trying to apply our own beliefs, experiences, knowledge and expertise to any given challenge. Unfortunately, this *"contribution blindness"* as I have come to call it, often means completely ignoring the experienced advice of those who have been successful and know a thing or two about getting it right. My advice here is simple and it's the only time I will ask you to do it. **Be lazy**. Accept that rules and guidance are there to help you reduce complexity, stress, uncertainty and risk, and should be taken or at least considered and capitalised upon at every available opportunity.

Now whilst ignorance may be bliss, it is no excuse for getting it wrong. So many great sources of advice, experience and knowledge exist there's really little or no excuse for not at least learning and applying the rules of the game. In many cases the rules of the game are simple and common sense but missing out a vital step or not following the advice and expertise forged by others will not only ensure that it's harder work than it needs to be, but also could, and often does, end in disaster. The thing about disasters is they don't announce they're coming. They can be catastrophic in nature and come along at the most inopportune times. Do not underestimate, trivialise or think that the basics are insignificant and not worthy of being followed. Greater entrepreneurs than you and I have failed miserably and unnecessarily along the startup journey because they simply did not follow the rules of the game. Don't make the same mistake. RTFM. If you don't know what that means, Google it.

7

THE PRACTICE OF LEARNING

I spend a lot of my time helping businesses to develop the capability to successfully lead, manage, support and deliver change and transformation across their organisations. One of the most common areas of failure is their inability to define, build and implement processes and systems that can be optimised and leveraged for success.

A common focus during my consulting engagements is helping businesses to implement lean and agile methodologies. If you are not familiar with these topics there is a ton of information and research material online. In short, lean and agile are based upon the principle of removing unnecessary wastage and minimising defects, whilst accelerating the delivery of value to customers. There are many disciplines, tools and practices within lean and agile methodologies but the one I am going to focus on here is called Kaizen. Kaizen simply means *"change for the better"*. Kaizen therefore focuses specifically on continuous improvement and is used to iteratively improve, optimise and leverage what you do and how you do it to deliver faster and more efficient results.

I am not going to go into great detail about Kaizen here, but I do want to focus on one principle that is helpful in understanding how you can improve what you do through the practice of learning. It also highlights my point about how insights and knowledge gained from direct learning experiences are the most valuable. Whilst the experiences, knowledge and expertise of others can help to flatten the learning curve somewhat there really is no substitute for in-depth personal learning experiences and practice. In the next principle I will cover the basics of building better processes using Kaizen principles.

8

MASTERY - SHU-HA-RI

The Power Of The Practiced Approach

Shu-Ha-Ri has its roots in Japanese martial arts, but the methodology has been adapted and adopted across a number of disciplines including agile and lean practices. Shu-Ha-Ri focuses on the systemised process of practiced learning to master any given task from the basics through to complete mastery. In essence Shu-Ha-Ri is the art of optimising, leveraging and refining processes through gained experience, learned knowledge and honed expertise. The high-level benefits of Shu-Ha-Ri (mastery) are:

Optimise processes to a level where as much unproductive superfluous wastage is removed as possible.

Reduce costs, risks, complexity and inefficiencies.

Accelerate defect-free productivity.

Create turnkey systems that produce repeatable predictable results.

The art of Shu-Ha-Ri, and yes, it is an art, is broken down into the following three core learning stages:

SHU

Shu is the first stage of attaining mastery within any given subject area. It's the starting point of approaching something brand new for the first time where you have little or no previous personal experience to draw on. For this example, I'm going to focus on building an Airfix model kit. The first time you undertake the task you will need to religiously follow the instructions to the letter (remember rules & guidelines), carefully and judiciously following each and every step as cautiously as possible. You start by reading the instructions carefully and then proceed to removing all of the parts from the plastic cut-outs. You lay them out and check each part against the contents list and then start to follow the build instructions step-by-step, exactly as directed. Your lack of experience and knowledge of the subject will mean that you are likely to make many mistakes along the way, even though you are following the build instructions and process to the letter. The first time you complete the task the investment in time and effort is likely to be disproportionately high to the delivered value, with the produced results likely being well below the desired standard. This is entirely normal and, as with learning anything new, your first attempts will more than likely be slow and clumsy. At this stage you will experience both the steepest learning curves and the most valuable learning opportunities for development and improvement. Once completed to a competent level where basic theories, concepts and implementation experience has been gained you will naturally enter into the second stage of Shu-Ha-Ri.

HA

The second stage of SHU-HA-RI mastery or **Ha** is where you have gained first-hand familiarity within a given subject, task or process. You may not be a master yet but you will have learned some basic lessons, understood the theory and now have the foundational experience needed to start optimising your approach and that of the build process. You now know everything you need to do before you start. You will be aware of the pitfalls and you may not even have to follow every step of the instructions to the letter, because you know how certain parts of the methodology and process work and in what order. At this stage you are more familiar and comfortable with completing the process, have developed your capability and are becoming more competent and confident in your ability to complete the given task successfully. You will also notice that you're getting faster and more efficient and that the quality of the end results are highly improved. At this point you're now quickly developing in-depth experience, knowledge and skills from immersion within the subject. At this stage the knowledge gained from building this type of "kit" is completely portable and can now be reused no matter what size or type of kit you choose to build in future. You know what needs to be done, you know how it should look and what you are looking to achieve, and you know the mechanics of getting it done efficiently. You will still refer to the instructions and manuals from time-to-time, but this will be more from a point of reference to confirm and validate your knowledge rather than materially needing them to build from. Once competency at this level is attained you will naturally move to the final stage of mastery.

RI

The final Shu-Ha-Ri transition to the **RI** stage is also the longest and is that of complete subject mastery. Achieving mastery within any discipline is when you have completed a given task or process so many times that your level of familiarity, experience and expertise becomes so great that you not only no longer need to refer to the manual but at this point you can rewrite the manual by developing your own approaches, methodologies and processes for completing the task based upon your own learned in-depth expertise and practice. Once mastery has been attained you are able to instantly see the bottlenecks and inefficiencies and are able to start to *"lean out"* and optimise the process whilst distilling it down to the absolute efficient minimum. Once you reach the RI stage of Shu-Ha-Ri you only do things that you really need to do in order to meet the objective and you will be able to minimise effort and time whilst maximising production rates and quality. It's at this stage where blueprints and turnkey processes can be developed which in turn can be automated and put on auto-pilot and work for you rather than you spending time working on them yourself. When you have reached mastery within any given subject or discipline you can start advising, training and providing consulting expertise to others who want to do likewise. Can you see how this simple three-step process can be leveraged to develop further revenue generating opportunities? Learning how to do something so well that you become the go to *"subject matter expert"* is where you can really start to differentiate yourself and truly stand out from the crowd.

9

Don't Underestimate Your Value

You're Special – Don't Underestimate That

You have probably always thought that you're special in some way? Well I'm here to tell you that your assumption is absolutely 100% correct.

So, it's official, you're special

Now I'm not telling you this because it's what you want to hear, nor do I tell you to stroke your ego or big you up in any way. I'm telling you this because like you, I struggled to startup my first ventures. I made countless mistakes along the way, lost money, lost hope at times and often just simply did not know where, when or how to get started. I did realise one thing early on though. If others were launching profitable *"on the side"* startups and becoming hugely successful at it, I instantly knew that it was possible for me to do the same, I just needed to figure out how.

> **Startup Pro Insight:** If something has already been successfully achieved by others that's all the evidence I need to confirm that it's possible for me. Want to know the easy way to reach any goal? Just ask one simple question. **What would need to be true for me to achieve it?** This simple

question exposes the foundations of **"what"** you need to do and **"how"**. Answering this one question is the easiest and quickest way to develop an effective ACTION plan.

I considered myself smart, hard-working and was committed, and after more than two decades of listening, learning, studying and, more importantly, doing, I discovered the one simple truth that made all the difference to my success and here it is:

Startup Pro Insight: I became an expert at separating the wheat from the chaff and focusing on achieving the most important things that gave me the results I needed.

I have hustled, taken risks, and put myself on the front line, but mostly I just got up and focused on getting the most important stuff done, and that's something you will discover along the way. If you're already out there doing it, you're not only a huge jump ahead of the competition but you have also assured your success, and I will tell you why. You are in the **very small minority** of people who will actually get up off the sofa, roll your sleeves up, commit to doing something and then follow it through to the end no matter what challenges confront you along the way. In fact you will embrace those challenges and turn them into opportunities. You possess unique talents, knowledge and experience that can be honed, leveraged and used to get you to where you want to be. The point is you got started and produced something that didn't exist yesterday, and that's when the magic really starts to happen.

Once you commit and get started you will rapidly build momentum and gain traction and that's when progress really starts to become exponential. You will quickly discover that starting your own enterprise is not the difficult to master dark art that many would have you believe. The fact is all you really need to get going is some good old-fashioned oomph and hustle.

Startup Pro Insight: Just get up and get started today. Waiting for tomorrow is an excuse.

By the way, when I say "today" that means right **NOW**. Not tomorrow or next week. In fact the power of **NOW** is so important that I'm going to ask you to make a commitment right now. Stop reading and go take the first step on creating your new enterprise. Make it something simple, quick and defining that puts a solid *"I have started"* stake in the ground. It could be as simple as registering your website's domain name, putting up a simple landing page, writing the first paragraph of a book, making a call or two, announcing it to the world on social media, booking in an appointment. Just make it an *"action step"* that defines the start and progresses you in some way on your journey. By the way, an *"action step"* needs to be something that's tangible, has an outcome and a result that signifies progress and most of importantly holds you accountable in some way. Perhaps that might mean a follow up, further calls, making a presentation, doing a demo or giving a talk.

10

SINK YOUR BIGGEST COMPETITOR

One of our worst flaws as people is our innate ability to be over-critical of ourselves, what we do and how we do it. We often find it difficult to put ourselves out on the front line without pulling our own work, ideas, dreams and aspirations to pieces. We are happy to highlight our flaws and almost take comfort in dismissing our own value. From our customer and clients' perspectives though they rarely see the chinks in the armour, and even if they do they are not likely to care.

Remember this: if you know just 1% more than your customers, you're better than most, 10% more and you're a true expert in their eyes, 50% more and you're an untouchable guru. In the real world we all have subject matter expertise that's hundreds, thousands and in many cases tens of thousands of percent more that our clients and that's why they hire us, buy our products and consume our services.

In simple terms you have skills, knowledge and answers to problems that they don't. One thing to remember, and I cover this in more detail later, is that if you're looking for perfectionism to provide you with a level of comfort you're happy with before you get started you're going to have a long unproductive wait.

Remember, Perfection Does Not Exist

Perfection, like a rainbow, is a complete illusion that does not exist as a defined state. Perfection is both dynamic in nature and highly subjective dependent upon your perspective. In my younger days I spent many years in the music industry and one of the most valuable pieces of advice I ever had bestowed upon me by a veteran professional was this.

> **Startup Pro Insight:** You may well know where the chinks in the armour are and where you made great howling mistakes, but don't ever feel compelled to point them out to your audience. Chances are they won't even have noticed.

I'm not saying that if things need improving not to improve them, what I am saying is don't get hung up on the *"perfection imperfection"* and most of all never let it prevent you from making progress.

> **Startup Pro Insight:** Here's a little secret to set you free from the **"perfection imperfection"**. Your biggest hurdle is not what you offer to the world, it's not what you know or what you don't, it's not about getting started, it's not about your finances, and it's not even about your competition. The biggest hurdle you will ever face in your quest for success is **YOU**.

The fact is that your competition fades into complete insignificance in comparison to the constraints and limitations you place upon yourself. Getting comfortable with yourself is one of the most important areas to master. I know some great academics, businesses people, inventors and sales people with massive potential. They could achieve true greatness, but guess what? They never come close to reaching their true potential because they never really commit to go *"all in"* and put themselves on the line. They fear failure, rejection, humiliation, being shown up or exposed as some kind of charlatan. Chances are you have had these exact feelings yourself from time-to-time, and that's ok because it's a really common feeling when you're starting anything new.

The easiest, fastest and most productive way of instantly expelling your old behaviours and negative ways of thinking and acting is to get some validation. When I first started out as a young musician I was terrified of singing in front of people. Every bone in my body was resistant to doing it. I thought I had no place in a well-established professional band with a large following. I let my mind run away with itself and I built catastrophic scenarios in my mind's eye where I would imagine being found out, humiliated and sacked on the spot, but then I thought, what have I got to lose? I dug deep and got on with it and literally overnight my whole perspective changed.

I was receiving great feedback about what a good singer I was from both the band members and the audience. I may not have been world class, a guru or even an expert but I did have enough validation from my customers that whatever I had was more than enough to get the job done in their eyes. I have applied this simple thinking on everything thing I have done since, and do you know what? I have never been humiliated, exposed as a fraud, or sacked.

> **Startup Pro Insight:** Take action NOW. Get out there and gain early validation that what you do and the results you deliver makes a massive difference to someone somewhere. This is the best way to position yourself,

quickly build confidence and will instantly change your perspective about how much value you can bestow on the world.

11

COST VS INVESTMENT

Success at anything doesn't just happen, it's not an event but a process. Success is the outcome of implementing well-defined processes that deliver the desired outcomes and results.

One of the biggest challenges facing new entrepreneurs is that starting up any new venture is very similar in nature to building a skyscraper. Let me explain that a little. To ensure that you end up with a solid structure which is capable of providing the required value you need to invest a lot of valuable time, effort and often money up front to create the **"*asset*"**. The challenge for many in the early days is that the investment in time, effort and money often delivers very little or nothing in the way of tangible results and returns. Just as with building the skyscraper, all the action is happening below the surface in the early days, with very little visible progress above ground. This is nearly always the stage where new entrepreneurs start giving up and falling by the wayside.

Here is the challenge. As people we crave instant gratification, we want to see results for our expended costs and efforts and we are very transactional in this respect. The result of this **"*instant gratification*"** mindset is that when we put in work and effort or spend money we expect an instant outcome and result to be delivered so that we may justify and possibly feel better about the cost. It's imperative that you change your thinking about **cost vs investment**. The time, money and effort spent early on in your startup should be viewed as the **investment** it is and not as a **cost**.

The difference between cost and investment is important to understand from a startup perspective as it materially changes your perspective from a mindset of *"instant gratification"* to one of long-term *value creation*. Let's take a look at the difference in mindsets between cost and investment. When you incur a cost (spend money) you automatically want and expect to see a quick direct tangible benefit or return.

> **I spend X and I receive Y** - A simple transaction of money or effort for perceived value in return. A straight retail purchase for example. Note: Costs (consumption) normally depreciate in value over time.
>
> With any investment however the realised benefit and return is a longer-term transaction with value delivered at some point in the future. For example:
>
> **I invest X now** and in X days/ months/ years I will receive a healthy return on my investment in excess of my initial investment.
>
> Note: Investments (creation) are designed to appreciate in value over time.

Whilst a number of different cost and investment models exist I am not going to discuss the different types and merits of each here. I have merely used two simple examples to highlight the differences in mindset from one of low value cost transaction to one of high value investment.

Successfully getting your enterprise up and running is not a cost based transactional event but the planned outcome of *investment* that will yield a healthy payback in future. Change your mindset from one of short-term cost driven gratification to one of purposeful longer-term investment and future value creation.

12

IDEAS NEED ACTION

Startup Pro Insight: Ideas are simply wistful thoughts, chemical reactions to conscious thought within your grey matter and that's exactly where they will stay if you do nothing with them. Your most important role as a budding entrepreneur is to take those ideas and turn them into reality.

Here are three of the most common questions I get asked during my startup mentoring and training sessions:

> **What are the best startup businesses?**
>
> **How do I come up with new ideas?**
>
> **How can I get more leads?**

I touch on the best types of startup businesses and lead creation later, but for now I want to concentrate on how to quickly and easily come up with great ideas for your *"on the side"* startups.

I know from experience that many entrepreneurs, especially new ones, can find it challenging to create startup ideas of their own. It's also common to find that the idea generation process itself is one of the hardest parts of any new venture. The truth is you're already an ideas expert, in fact you do it all the time. Let me quickly demonstrate how you're already an idea creation machine worth a fortune.

> How frequently do you voice your opinions about how a service or product could be improved? **Idea creation** - Improve the service or product.

> How often do you say things like "why don't they do X or Y?". **Idea creation** - Go and do it.

> "How simple would it be for them just to add X?". **Idea creation** - Add the X factor that's missing.

> What about, "I've had a great idea to help the X industry". **Idea creation** - Go help the X industry implement your great idea.

> Or the armchair CEO view, "If I was running that company I'd make sure that we implemented X". **Idea creation** - Set up your own company with X implemented or share your ideas with the company in question. You will be amazed at how opportunities can develop from simple conversations.

My point is that every one of us has perspectives, views and opinions on what others are doing and how they are doing it. This includes how it could be changed or improved. My bet is that if I gave you a problem to solve right now you would go away and think about it for a while, perhaps you might even carry out some in-depth research, and as a result you would return to me in a couple of days' time bubbling with ideas and a range of solutions and options for me to consider. That's the entrepreneurial mind creating ideas, innovations and improvements right there.

I have made a substantial second income over the years doing nothing more than going to businesses with my ideas about how they could be improving what they do and how they do it. I have suggested everything from small soft innovations, different ways of working, to new products and services. I then offer to help them execute and implement those ideas. I have zero overheads other than my time, and importantly do not need to invest my own resources to develop products or services to make a profit. Added to which I am completely devoid of risk. I am an ideas creation agency needing nothing more than a keen eye, basic investigative skills and the imagination to create ideas. This method of helping organisations to progress is a completely legitimate *"on the side"* micro startup business model in its own right, and one that I have been successfully leveraging for years.

All businesses are mad, crazy and hungry for new ideas and resolutions to their problems and will happily pay you well for helping them to define, develop and deliver them. Ideas really are in abundance, they are everywhere you look. Another great way of quickly exposing unexplored opportunities is to listen carefully to how people speak around you. Learning how to tune into peoples' language is a sure-fire way of quickly identifying plain sight problems that can be translated into income and profits. Look out for words such as: *painful, inconvenient, constraint, limiting, limited, trouble, time consuming, costly, expensive, slow, complicated, manual, laborious.* These types of words all suggest ripe opportunities waiting to be acted upon.

The real problem as you will soon discover is not in generating, creating and defining ideas and solutions, that part as I have demonstrated is in fact relatively easy to achieve. One thing that separates wannapreneurs from the real deal is this:

Execution & Implementation

Or more simply put, having the ability to turn those casual thoughts and ideas into real tangible offerings that matter to a defined group of customers. Learn to master the process of execution and implementation well and you will be way ahead of the crowd and certainly on your way to becoming a true startup pro.

13

GET A TEACHER

When undertaking new projects and learning new skills it can become apparent very quickly that enthusiasm and motivation can only get you so far before you reach a plateau and start to experience a serious slump in ongoing progress and performance. The quickest and most reliable way to get over this hump is to get yourself an experienced teacher, coach or mentor and become an avid student. I know that many of you may resist doing this because you believe that your own intellect, smarts and academic proficiency is enough to succeed. The desperately misguided belief that raw intelligence, academic ability and business savvy adds up to congruent subject matter expertise is a common one which both individuals and businesses fall foul of. This limited way of thinking not only thwarts potential, it's what keeps the average and mediocre average and mediocre.

> **Startup Pro Insight:** Common sense, IQ and academic qualifications do not equate to subject matter expertise, for that you need learning and experience of application.

Going it alone without help and guidance for any length of time will result in you naturally reaching, and more importantly maintaining, a certain level of competency whereby you will continue to do the same things, use the same skills and continue to make the same mistakes.

This is all part of the natural organic learning process but will always restrict your progress and performance within the confines and comfort of your current capabilities.

When I first started learning to play the guitar, I spent a huge amount of time and effort judiciously teaching myself the basics. I learned how to play chords, progressions and then finally a number of songs, eventually developing my skills to a proficient general playing style, I even managed a few fairly impressive solos. In the beginning progress was swift and over time improvements in my performance were evident. After a couple of years however my progress dramatically stalled and I found myself applying the same knowledge, playing patterns and techniques over and over again. The trouble was I was seeing virtually no progress, everything was starting to sound the same and, more importantly, others around were seemingly making far more progress, securing better engagements and higher paying gigs. At that point I decided to get a teacher to start building upon my basic learning, honing my skills and expanding my technical knowledge. Within weeks my playing ability, repertoire and confidence had soared and the rest as they say is history. My experience of engaging professionals to help me progress my position and increase my capability has stuck with me ever since, and I continue to seek professional coaching and mentoring when and wherever needed.

It's important to point out that eliciting the help of a subject matter expert in person may not always be possible or indeed practical although it's the best method for fast progress and personal accountability. Teaching, coaching and mentoring for you however might be as simple as reading some books, taking an online course or joining a professional group or association. The key thing to remember here is that your results will be always limited to what you know. It's a simple equation. The more you know, the more performant you will become, which in turn translates into improved results. Take a look at anyone who's been successful, TV personalities, writers, actors, entrepreneurs and public figures, my bet is you will find a great teacher, coach or mentor who has helped them to achieve and perform at their best. If you're serious about what you do, make the investment to get the help you need to get there. The results can be truly life changing.

14

Define Important

Startup Pro Insight: I'm going to be honest with you now and cut through all the distracting noise that surrounds the startup process. Launching and delivering a tangible product or service to real paying customers is the quickest most effective way of becoming successful that I know of. It trumps all analytics, assumptions and modelling. Yes, it's a pretty basic principle but a pocket full of money is the only proof I ever need that something is working.

What's The Problem?

The reality in the startup world is that the majority become bogged down with the unimportant minutiae and lose sight of the two things that are really important, which are: delivering value to clients and generating enough revenue to live, thrive and survive, and doing both as quickly as possible.

So why do so many startup entrepreneurs get tied up in low-level and non-essential work that delivers very little?

The reasons for this are as wide and varied as those who suffer from the problem in the first place. Here are just a few of the most common hurdles that stop new startup entrepreneurs in their tracks.

For some it's simply a lack of knowledge or experience of how to really get something up and running quickly. Education however is cheaply and often freely available. There really is little reason not to be able to find good expert resources such as coaches, mentors and trainers who can help you fill in the missing gaps.

For others it's just about lacking the confidence to launch and get something out to customers, fearing failure, rejection and ultimately loss. Emotions play a big part here and most new entrepreneurs aren't comfortable with putting their precious **"baby"** in the firing line. Taking criticism, even if it's constructive, can be difficult, but learning to reframe it as an opportunity to learn, improve and do things better is worth its weight in gold.

Some entrepreneurs just suffer from what I call "blind vision". Blind vision is the obsessive phenomenon whereby you have defined a crystal-clear vision of the perfect product or service, which of course is understandable; why would you think any differently if you're building it in your mind's eye? The problem with this unmovable mindset is that you will make it virtually impossible for yourself to ever satisfy the **"vision"**. You will continually be using your perfect vision view as the **"success"** metric by which all progress, performance and quality is measured. Now don't get me wrong, having an objective to deliver the best possible products and services you possibly can is what you should be aspiring to, but that comes later down the line once you have validated your ideas, have engaged your **"interested audience"** and are providing a solution that delivers the desired outcome and results.

A simple technique that I use to great effect to keep *"blind vision"* at bay is this. I define three transitional versions of my vision that I reference throughout the different stages of the startup process.

> **Firstly, I have the perfect vision.** This is the aspirational perfect world version of my offering. I use this as a baseline to mark long-term progress, define strategies and measure evolution. I do not use this to validate early hypotheses or assumptions, or as my short-term delivery benchmark.
>
> **Then, I have my target vision.** This is where I am headed in the medium-term. This is the end game after the initial launch and is the desired transitional state derived after initial customer feedback.
>
> **Lastly, I have the "startup vision" or the Minimum Viable Product.** This is a somewhat diluted base version of the aspirational **"perfect vision"** but one that can be produced and tested as quickly and as cost effectively as possible. This is your experimental hypothesis proving model and the first stage of your venture. This is where the **"scientist"** entrepreneur does his finest work.

15

SIMPLICITY BREEDS EFFECTIVENESS

We have all heard the phrase **K**eep **I**t **S**imple **S**tupid or **KISS** for short. When you boil it down, successfully starting a new *"on the side"* venture can be distilled down into a **KISS** based checklist approach. I have developed this simple startup plan that I use for all of my startups. This is not meant to be a definitive process and depending upon your business type, structure and particular offerings it may differ somewhat and need to be adapted, but in general these are the essential *"must do"* elements involved.

A Simple Startup Framework

The Challenge - Clearly define the problem to be resolved.

Target Market - Identify the audience with the problem and understand why resolving it matters to them.

Idea Creation - Generate as many ideas, options & hypothetical solutions that solve the problem as effectively as you can.

Experimentation - Design experiments to prove or disprove your hypothesis (develop and build your Minimum

Viable Product or service offering based upon the option(s) that best meet your customers' needs).

Testing - Carry out hypothetical tests - experiment and test your MVP with real customers in order to capture enough data to derive the insights needed to prove or disprove your hypothesis whilst validating assumptions and ascertaining both feasibility and viability.

Measure Everything - Measure & validate results against defined success criteria.

Iterate & Retest - Continuous iteration of your products and services based upon your measured results and associated customer feedback.

The Outcome - Happy customers.

The Result - You get paid.

In short, just give your customers what they want and keep improving what you do until you get there.

Once you learn to focus on this simple startup process you will quickly discover how effective you can become in a relatively short space of time. If you're one of the growing number of people who want to startup and run their own business but are permanently putting back the launch date, are unable to release products due to them being *"not quite ready"* or find yourself forever tweaking, reworking or re-planning then the chances are you are suffering from what's known as *"launch paralysis"*.

A regular challenge I see new startup entrepreneurs facing is their continual propensity to overthink, overcomplicate and overanalyse everything down to the nth degree. The problem with this approach is that whilst thinking and modelling a raft of scenarios can be extremely beneficial for coming up with ideas, solving complex problems and making more accurate decisions, it does have the unfortunate and significant downside of preventing action being taken. Even the great Sir Isaac Newton who used logical modelling extensively had problems in articulating that into actionable steps. In his case this meant designing and building experiments to prove his theories, in fact he employed others to help him design and carry out experiments to prove his theories. Yes, the devil may be in the detail but in the beginning it's all about taking enough action to get results and feedback. The real detail and thinking comes once you have some gained some initial data and insights to work with.

16

DEFINE, DEVELOP & DELIVER

I have referenced the term **Minimum Viable Product or Service** several times already so let's take a closer look at what that is, its purpose and how it's going to prevent you from making some costly and time-consuming mistakes. A Minimum Viable Product or *MVP* is a bare bones version of your offering that provides just enough features, functionality and benefits that potential customers will be willing to put their hand in their pockets and pay for. Nothing more and nothing less.

Remember the *"startup vision"* I mentioned in the last chapter, the diluted quick and cheap version of your aspirational vision. Any more than the minimum required at this early stage and you're jumping the gun, making critical assumptions about the features and benefits that your clients may want. Any less and you risk not offering enough value for them to part with their hard-earned cash.

Your **Minimum Viable Product** does not include all the bells and whistles of your ideal aspirational product or service, and that's by design. All of the shine and polish gets added down the line once you have gained feedback from your early adopters as to what needs to be included to make it highly valuable from their perspective.

Startup Pro Insight: keep in mind that needs and wants are two very different things, but your customers will want both satisfied. It's only the proportion of each that varies.

The idea in the very early stages is to launch as quickly and as cost effectively as possible while delivering something of value to your market that will start generating revenue. Launching early enables you to quickly test and validate your ideas and assumptions (remember the scientist approach). It also provides you with the opportunity to elicit valuable insights into what your customers and clients really find valuable, or not, and what problems they really need solving as a priority. Being able to meet growing customer demands quickly is a very effective method for gaining much needed early momentum, traction and of course revenue.

It's a fact that many businesses discover untapped channels, markets and opportunities in the early post launch days. These are opportunities that would never have been exposed if it were not for getting something out the door and seeking early customer feedback. Once the initial launch has been done it's imperative that the voice of your customers drives the development and delivery of future benefits. Early customers are the best source of information about your market, industry and types of features and functionality they find valuable. Most customers enjoy interaction and contribution and won't be shy in coming forward to share their opinions with you. Be warned, you may not like everything you hear, but then again that's the point.

Taking notice of your buyers is the quickest way for you to add value, develop compelling offers and build your customers' trust and loyalty. You will however need to develop an effective feedback system for monitoring responses, qualifying results and capturing data. You will also need to be able to track emerging customer requirements against future development cycles.

What is it you need.... exactly?

Being clear and decisive about what you need to do in order to launch your **Minimum Viable Product** (MVP) or service is critical. Prioritising just what you need to get done to have a product or service that you can charge for is where you should be aiming. No matter how much you plan to invest in or develop your offerings, the chances are that you may need to pivot your approach. In the early days you may even end up identifying and targeting new or peripheral markets you had not even contemplated as opportunity hotspots. Be ready for that and accept that your business, its operating model and even what you do and how may need to change significantly to hit its sweet spot.

Why Change?

The need for change means that your business is *evolving* to meet real customer needs rather than relying on assumptive guesswork, and that's a good thing. It's important to remember that your own opinions and viewpoints will only get you so far. Being open to criticism, advice, and requests is an imperative part of sustaining your long-term value and differentiation in the marketplace. Many fledgling entrepreneurs look at criticisms from customers as a personal attack, when in fact it's a point of frustration that's born out of interest, and interest my friends is where sales are made. How many times have you found yourself frustrated with a product or service that you love except for one or two small niggles. You want to use it, but you're just disgruntled that it's not quite where you need it to be. When the opportunity arises take the criticisms proactively, they provide direction for future successes.

Startup Pro Insight: Remember that your job as an entrepreneur is really quite simple. It's to solve problems better than anyone else can. The better and more efficiently you solve these problems and improve the client's condition, the more value you're adding. The size and impact of the problem has a direct correlation to the amount of revenue and profit you can generate.

17

LAUNCH & TEST YOUR MVP

As soon as you have developed your Minimum Viable Product or Service to a level where it delivers enough value that your clients will pay for -

Launch it.

I don't want to labour the point here, but it's an important one to get nailed at this early stage. You are not looking to launch a completed and polished product or service at this point. You are simply trying to evaluate what your clients find desirable, what they will be happy paying for, and of course determine how much.

One of the most valuable entrepreneurial lessons I have learned over the years is that the vast majority of your most important learning, value-add and customer insights happens after you launch and not before. Resist the almost compulsive temptation to take years to build your perfect masterpiece in total silence and isolation behind closed doors. I know entrepreneurs who have developed products and services in this way only to discover that the opportunity was long gone, they had no sustainable market, or their offering was not commercially viable in the first place.

Startup Pro Insight: New entrepreneurs often fall foul of the perceived glitz and glamour of being a new shiny startup and forget their real purpose. In the beginning forget about the startup razzmatazz and start thinking, acting and performing like a scientist. Your role as an entrepreneur is to be consistently coming up with new hair-brained ideas, and then defining models, building prototypes, and developing tests and experiments to prove and validate those conditions and assumptions. Changing your thinking to that of the scientist often results in different perspectives, allows a much more agile approach and ultimately ensures you only commit your scarce resources to validated ideas that have an outside chance of generating value and revenue.

18

LEARN TO LISTEN

There is a reason why you have two ears and only one mouth. It's so you can listen twice as much as you talk. Failure to launch quickly and capture the voice of your customer could mean spending valuable time, money and effort coming up with products or services that you think are the perfect solution to a given problem, only to discover that one of the following conditions is true:

You're offering a solution to a problem that no one really has.

You have no audience or market to begin with.

The target market is so small that any sustainable profitability is impractical.

The business model is totally unviable.

The halls of business history are littered with these sorts of failures. You want answers to these questions as quickly and as cheaply as you possibly can. That way you can quickly pivot should you need to.

19

EXPECT TO PIVOT

For those of you unaware of what the term *pivoting* refers to, it's a point where a startup discovers that its initial offering, market and sometimes both are not ***who***, ***what*** or ***where*** they first thought. Businesses often uncover additional market opportunities that were only exposed after the initial launch and were never identified in the first instance. They then pivot or turn the business around as quickly as possible to adapt, focus and develop products or services to fulfil and leverage the newly identified opportunity and associated target market.

Again, can you start to see the benefits of being agile and launching as quickly and cheaply as you can?

A common question I get asked is "How do you know when you're ready to launch?" I like to take LinkedIn founder Reid Hoffman's approach on this one. Reid famously said:

"If you're not embarrassed by the first version of your product, you've launched too late."

20

RISK IS UNAVOIDABLE

Anyone who has ever started up a new venture or aspired to do so will tell you that it's a high-risk proposition peppered with uncertainty. On the face of it they are, of course, absolutely right. Now that's perhaps not what you wanted to hear at this point but by and large it's true. On the face of it your shiny new enterprise is dependent upon so much having to go right, alongside the vast probability that so much can and probably will go wrong. Statistics alone will tell you that the odds are not in your favour. So how can you overcome the inevitable risks along the way? One thing I do is to view everything with a project management mindset. No matter what that project is, what it delivers, to whom, why and how, it attracts risk by the bucket load. To think any differently is naive at best and reckless at worst. The thing about risk is that it has a direct correlation and proportional impact based upon a number of key variables that can be segregated into two distinct groups:

Group 1 (Minimising)

Minimising the following key areas will significantly reduce risk:

Size, Uniqueness, Complexity, Uncertainty

Group 2 (Maximising)

Maximising the following key areas will also significantly reduce risk:

Knowledge, Experience, Expertise, Predictability, Capability

With this in mind it would make sense that large, unique and complex projects delivered over short timescales would attract the greatest risk. On the other hand, small simple well-defined projects where predictability and capability to deliver alongside adequate timescales would reduce that project's risk profile significantly. Trying to start up big complex projects and doing it quickly is difficult and therefore attracts higher risk. Small, well-defined projects with clear outcomes that can be deployed quickly, easily and with minimal risk on the other hand have a far better rate of successful delivery. Suffice to say that keeping your startup projects **Quick, Small and Simple** (QSS) will dramatically reduce and in some cases completely mitigate your ETR or **Exposure To Risk.**

21

MINIMISING YOUR ETR

Minimising your **ETR** or **E**xposure **T**o **R**isk is important for any business, but it's far more important for the fragile startup. **ETR** has three key areas that you can focus on for mitigating risk. For the purpose of this chapter, risks are defined as events that could happen, whilst issues are defined as risks that have actually happened.

Reducing the probability of risk occurring in the first place.

Reducing the time that you are exposed to any given risk.

Reducing the size and impact of a risk should it become an issue.

Reducing your ETR will not only keep you on the right side of sanity, it will also ensure that your business operations develop a resistance to risk whilst developing robust processes for managing issues effectively when they do occur. Putting all your eggs into one basket is one thing, but putting all your eggs into an unknown basket is something else entirely. It's impossible to entirely avoid risk of course, but you can manage it more effectively by setting up systems and processes for dealing with it when it does present itself. Keep the following in mind. There are a limited number of ways to manage risk and issues, including the following:

Mitigate: Minimising risks and associated impacts

Resolve: Removing the root cause of the risk or issue

Defer: Removing the immediate risk & or deferring its impact

Delegate: Moving a risk to someone or somewhere else

Ignore: Low or no impact –No action required

Accept: Accept probability of a risk occurring alongside the likely impacts

Dismiss: The risk has little or no direct impact

Increase: Increasing one risk to lessen the impact of another

Risk management experts have a whole raft of tools, principles and methodologies for *"accurately"* weighting and assessing risks, their impacts and probabilities. As with most things the most effective way to manage and mitigate risk is to keep it as simple and as straightforward as possible. I use the following simple pragmatic principles for managing risk.

> **Accept that risks and issues will happen.** Accept that risks and subsequent issues will generate unwanted and often undesirable challenges and results that will need to be managed effectively.
>
> **Expect that risks and issues will happen.** Working on the principle that forewarned is forearmed, expecting the worst gives you the resilience needed to deal with them quickly and effectively.

Define the worst possible outcome. This principle works on the assumption that no one is going to die as a result of the risk and it's never going to be as bad as you think (there are exceptions of course but life-threatening risks require a whole different approach and that's not something I'm going to cover here). It may be that you lose a little money, some time, or even, shock horror, some pride, but once you have defined and accepted the worst possible outcome you can start to examine and investigate potential solutions to resolve them ahead of time. Having a procedure and approach to manage risk, issues and associated impacts effectively is far more valuable than trying to plan for every eventuality on the planet, which of course you can't.

Spend 10% of the time evaluating the risk and 90% of the available time working on a solution, not the other way around. Many spend 90% of their time going over and over the problem and little time on its actual resolution. The trick is to work on mitigating problems, risks and challenges as much as you can without stifling your creativity or ability to progress towards your goals and the ultimate outcomes.

Choose which risk management strategy to use for best effect. Mitigate, Resolve, Defer, Delegate, Ignore, Accept, Dismiss, Increase. And yes, in some circumstances you may choose to increase a risk if it helps to meet your objectives. For example, if you need to get your new product or service to market quickly in order to beat your competition to the line and doing so gains you a competitive position, increasing your risk may be a valid proposition especially if it's in the short-term and can be managed adequately.

22

Plan, But Not Too Much

While outline strategic planning is of course needed to provide purpose and direction, too much can be detrimental and disruptive to progress. The problem with planning is that it's largely based upon guesswork about potential future outcomes, with little focus on the here and now. Spending time over-planning or *"crystal ball gazing"* just ensures that you will spend your most creative time pondering what you think you may need to do in future rather than actually doing what you need to do today. Having a clear focus on what needs to be done today to make tangible progress is far more constructive and valuable than wasting months on never-ending planning. Remember that planning is an abstract concept and should never be confused with execution and application.

In short, spend the minimum amount of time on planning and the maximum amount of time actively testing your ideas and assumptions. Over-planning is for talkers, action is for walkers.

"Planning is an abstract concept and should never be confused with execution and application."

23

DITCH YOUR EXCUSES

Many would-be entrepreneurs start off with good intentions, great ideas and buckets of enthusiasm but fail to follow it through to a profitable conclusion. This phenomenon however is not exclusive to business startups, it happens in virtually every area of our lives. How many projects, diets or exercise regimes have you started and failed to finish? In fact how many books, films or blog posts have you started but never finished? It's prevalent everywhere and the reason for this constant loop of startup and stall is simply because you don't have a big enough why. The chances are you love the idea of running your own show or developing additional income streams on the side but you don't want to pay the price to get there. YET.

The symptoms of the staller are easy to spot. If you find yourself putting off making a start or coming up with never-ending excuses or delaying tactics, are constantly missing deadlines or using tomorrow as your starting point then the chances are you're lacking commitment, investment, drive, motivation or purpose. Committed entrepreneurs however will not allow procrastination to win the day. Winners move themselves to action, are motivated beyond belief, exude enthusiasm and are constantly focused on actions that progress them towards their goals. They are fuelled by excitement, interest and a never-ending supply of drive and purpose for what they do and what they stand for.

You will often find the most successful people live and breathe their vocation, they are on an uncompromising mission to change the world, or the lives of the people in it.

If you're not invested in what you're doing it's never going to be a success. **Tomorrow is not a plan, it's an excuse.** If you constantly find yourself in excuse mode rather than one of action I would strongly suggest that you take some time to evaluate what you're doing and your why.

24

CLARITY & VISION

Your strategies and tactics are the fundamental building blocks of the value you deliver

Being clear about your strategies and tactics is a critical element for any successful entrepreneur. They clearly define your objectives and outcomes and map out exactly what needs to be done, when, and by whom, to achieve the desired results. They also provide the basis for defining success criteria and the key performance indicators or KPIs needed to measure progress and results. Many people make the mistake of using the terms strategy and tactics interchangeably, when in fact they have very different meanings. Strategies are your top priorities and goals. These are the objectives and outcomes that once reached will produce the desired results. Tactics on the other hand are the mechanics of how you will deliver those outcomes and results.

Strategies define clear objectives, outcomes and results.

Tactics are the steps and actions taken to meet your objectives and deliver the desired outcomes and results.

The easy way to understand and demonstrate how strategies and tactics work in practice is to look at how armies execute their plans during battles. The strategy may be defined as the following objective and result: *"Regain control of a specific area"*. This outcome is defined well before any specific action is considered or taken. Tactics define **the mechanics of how** that specific objective and result will be achieved. Outline tactics, like strategies, will also be defined before any action is taken but it's important to remember that tactics are only *executed* once the battle has commenced and will be subject to constant monitoring, re-evaluation and on the fly adjustments to accommodate changing circumstances as the battle unfolds. That's why it's important to ensure that your strategies and tactics are constantly aligned. Any differentiation or misalignment between the two may prove detrimental to the successful delivery of the desired outcome.

It's really common for organisations and individuals alike to fail to put this into practice. They will often find themselves changing their strategies and objectives along the way but failing to adjust their tactical approach and then wondering why they did not achieve the expected outcomes and results. Successful execution of your strategies and tactics relies upon great communication at every level. If your communication mechanisms are poor, it's extremely difficult to keep both your strategies and tactics aligned while in progress.

> **Startup Pro Insight:** Real business strategies are easy to qualify with two simple criteria:
>
> The outcome of your strategies really matters to your customers.
>
> Your strategies differentiate you from your competition. Make sure though that your differentiation also matters to your clients. It's no good making your product cheaper or

twice the size if your all your customers care about is the speed of delivery.

25

BE SPECIFIC

You are more than likely familiar with **SMART** goals, but if not, it's a great place to start for keeping your startup efforts on track. The **SMART** acronym stands for:

Specific, **M**easurable, **A**ctionable, **R**ealistic, **T**ime-bound

SMART goals will help you to supercharge your productivity and keep you focused. So when you are setting your goals, strategies and objectives, make sure that they follow the SMART framework. Questions you might like to ask when defining your goals might include:

What will I achieve? - **Exactly**

When will I achieve it? - **Precisely**

What does the outcome look like? - **Specifically**

How am I going to achieve it? – **In step by step detail**

What does success look like? - **Again in specific detail**

How will I measure success? - **Clearly defined metrics**

What is the timeline? - **Again define every detail**

Define how you are going to measure progress and success. Setting objectives and goals is great but if you cannot measure progress and results it's pointless. All goals and outcomes must be realistic, specific and achievable. Setting a defined timeline for goals will also ensure that you remain focused and accountable for their completion.

26

MOVE YOUR MOUNTAINS

Being able to move your particular mountain requires many interrelated elements to work together but if you want a simple framework for becoming successful at anything here it is:

> Define your purpose
>
> Make the commitment
>
> Maintain clear focus
>
> Take massive action
>
> Be consistent

Defining a clear **purpose** and then **committing** to **consistently** taking **focused action** can quite literally move mountains.

27

KEEP TO THE DEADLINE

Similar to the time-bound component of **SMART goals,** defining an achievable deadline is so important because it's often one of most overlooked and neglected areas on any project. Unlike a timeline that measures progress and the duration of a project, a deadline is an unmovable milestone that must be met and cannot be moved.

> Set a deadline that's achievable and stick to it like glue.

I mean it. Do not postpone it, move it or let anything encroach on it. If you let that happen you will continuously delay your launch because there is always something that's perceived as more important waiting in the wings to throw a spanner in the works, if you let it.

28

KEEP FOCUSED ON THE FINISH LINE

The world is full of enthusiastic starters, but it could do with a few more enthusiastic finishers.

Starting something is a milestone and hard enough on its own, but so many potential startup pioneers will fail to complete what they started and never cross the finish line.

Despite what you may think, starting work on a new project is actually the easy part. Look at it this way, at the outset you have the motivation, purpose and vision which is driven by raw excitement and the will to achieve something great. Once you are actively working on your project however it's inevitable that momentum will start to wane once you start experiencing some challenges, have a setback or two, or face the realisation that you have been hard at work for months with little or nothing to show for it. You may have even had challenges, knock backs and disappointments that have made you doubt your product, service or even your own abilities, knowledge and credentials.

These are normal emotions and I would say are a necessary part of your journey, but you must ride this wave and keep focused on delivering the vision. Getting started is the easy part, real entrepreneurial strength comes from the resilience you develop and apply to your efforts over time. You can help to build this resilience by regularly reaffirming what it is you are doing and why. Be clear and specific about your daily, weekly and monthly goals. Know your objectives and keep a clear focus on what the outcome looks like, and how the results will benefit your customers and clients. Be clear about how each significant milestone impacts your progress and moves your venture forward. Remember anything that does not provide a tangible movement forwards is wasted effort. Keep your momentum and commitment high by consistently qualifying your top priorities and making sure they are:

Important - Enables progress

Urgent - Has to happen for progress to be made

Significant - Delivers measurable results that move you towards your goals

Startup Pro Insight: know what the end goal looks like but don't focus on it so much that you negate to carry out the hands-on work needed to successfully achieve it.

29

DON'T PLAY IT SAFE

How many times have you heard someone saying, ***"I'm playing it safe"***, or ***"It's the safest option"***. My bet is that you hear it all the time. In fact the reality is that you're more than likely the one doing most of the talking when you hear those words.

> **Startup Pro Insight:** Playing it safe, taking the safe option, or heading off down the safe route will do one thing and one thing only. It will absolutely guarantee that you will get exactly the same tomorrow as you have today. That's fine of course if what you have now is exactly what you want. For most of us however that's not the case. If you want to change what tomorrow looks like and get different results you're going to need to venture into the unknown and be prepared to take on the feelings of discomfort and risk, because that's where the gold is.

Do you think that life's winners, the wealthy, the most successful and those living their dream lifestyles play it safe? No of course not, they accept the direct correlation between risk taken and reward gained. The most successful people balance risk by learning how to manage and mitigate it effectively but most of all they accept that it's part of the game. The fact is that those playing it safe are the same 95% of the herd that you're trying to break free from. If that's not enough of an incentive to accept the risk and take some action I don't know what is.

30

COMFORT IS NOT YOUR FRIEND

We all know that practice makes perfect. The more we do something the better we get at it (remember developing mastery with Shu-Ha-Ri). We also know that the more we do something the more comfortable and routine it becomes, but that's not always a good thing. Comfort may make us feel emotionally safe and secure, but becoming overly comfortable can, and often does, lead to us accepting a certain level of complacency which in turn can hinder creativity and dumb down our thinking. More importantly though it can stop you from taking the uncomfortable roads where opportunities are greatest.

> **Startup Pro Insight:** If you are not uncomfortable with a high proportion of what you're doing on a daily, weekly or monthly basis then you're probably not doing enough of what really counts.

I cannot stress this point strongly enough. My biggest opportunities, successes and wins have all meant having to overcome some very uncomfortable thoughts, emotions and actions. But I will tell you one thing; I would much rather be uncomfortable taking control and making the changes needed to achieve success than being uncomfortable with someone else being in charge and making those decisions for me.

31

FEAR THE HIGHWAYMAN

Turn fear into fuel or it will rob you of the life you should have had.

I know some wildly successful entrepreneurs who have all had great ideas, genius inspiration and the aspiration to achieve greatness and leave their mark on the world. These prolific creators are in the same league as the Edisons, the Newtons, and the Jobs of this world. They are the innovators, disruptors and pioneers of the future. They all have an infectious passion for what they do, love life, have masses of positive energy and live lives that most can only dream of. They have all built massive businesses and incomes, have touched the lives of millions and given generously to charities and foundations. These entrepreneurial masters have amassed billions between them and quite literally live the utopian entrepreneurial dream. Well at least that's the life they could have had if they had not let fear quite literally steal their future lives right from under them.

Fear will not only limit your abilities in the present, it's a rot that will rob you of the future life that's just waiting to be achieved. Many great books have been written on the subject of fear, what it is, and how best to conquer or at the very least manage it effectively, so I will not be covering that in great detail here. What I am going to do is give you some simple pointers for managing fear and converting it into fuel that can be used for motivation and action rather than discomfort and procrastination.

Here are two of the best strategies I know of for dealing with fear. Master these and you will be well on your way to changing your mindset and your future forever:

> **Strategy 1: Expect It**- Expecting anything allows you to do something really valuable. It forewarns and forearms. It allows you to prepare a state of readiness and build the capability to manage for any eventuality. Being mentally prepared for and having a plan to deal with fear when it does rear its ugly head will enable you to stop the panic, procrastination and ultimately defeat. Having a process for managing fear also helps you to embrace and reframe it with more perspective and objectivity, and in doing so allows to you to use it as a positive emotion rather than a negative one.
>
> **Strategy 2: Accept It** – Let's get one thing straight; you cannot stop fear from occurring. Fear is a natural built in emotion and it's one of our primary safety mechanisms for directing us away from danger. Fear and the situations that generate it for you are always going to happen, it's how you respond to those events that matter. Once you make the simple mindset shift of accepting that fear will happen you will instantly become much more objective about managing it effectively.

Strategy 3: Check If It's Real - My next fear coping strategy deals with the emotional and logical side of our thinking. Ask yourself this question when faced with fear:

Is what I fear real or perceived?

Using Pareto's 80/20 law, most fears that we worry about are perceived constructs that we build internally. How many times have you heard someone say, *"That was not as bad as I was expecting"*? What's really being said is that the perceived fear generated in their mind's eye was much more daunting than the real event.

People often say that their biggest fears never happen.

One important question to ask yourself when you feel fear taking hold is *"Am I dealing with a real fear or a perceived one?"* Our feelings of fear are often exacerbated when we focus on visualised scenarios of what could happen rather than what actually happens. This is known as catastrophic thinking. Some people have even developed a fear of fear itself and in doing so create a never-ending loop of anxiety, worry and unease. It's important to understand your fears alongside the associated emotional feelings, triggers and underlying causes before they start to detrimentally influence what you do as a result.

When you start looking at fear logically many of our darkest fears are not real at all and are internally generated by us. Susan Jeffers in her great book *"Feel the Fear and Do it Anyway"* said that one of the key ways of dealing with fear is to *"know that you will deal with it, whatever it is"*. In my experience that's been pretty sound advice. In any given situation there are only so many options for dealing with fear and they are as follows:

Manage it

Remove it

Accept it

I am going to let you into a little secret about fear right now that has helped many instantly dispel their fears completely; and here it is.

Fear is actually just a lack of knowledge

I am not advocating that deep-seated phobias can be eradicated easily, because fears and phobias are not the same thing and have significant differences, both in their root causes and methods of managing the emotional impacts and effects. But you may find it useful to start thinking about fear differently by using a simple reframing method.

Instead of saying *"I have a fear of X"*, turn that around and say *"I have a lack of knowledge about X"*. The upside of this simple mindset shift is that becoming educated about something is relatively quick, simple and easy.

The Simplest Ways Of Dealing With Fear

Validation: Is the fear real or perceived?

Education: As I said, many fears are based upon a lack of knowledge. Educating yourself and calling upon the experiences of others is a great way of alleviating the anxieties and uncomfortable feelings associated with fear.

Identification: What is the worst possible outcome?

Action: Define what actions you would need to take to improve the condition.

Acceptance: Accept the situation and work with it knowing that whatever it is you can deal with it.

32

GETTING QUICK RESULTS

Focus is the ultimate secret weapon of the most effective, productive and wealthy entrepreneurs. Focusing on just one thing at a time however is one of those *"looks simple to do"* kind of things but is far more difficult to achieve in practice. Difficult or not, developing the ability to maintain a solid focus in one specific area at a time is a skill you absolutely must master if you want to become a successful entrepreneur.

Despite what many people believe, think or may have told you, we are just plain poor at multitasking. Now I know there are those who use multitasking as some kind of badge of honour to demonstrate their prowess at just how great they are at juggling *"lots of stuff "*, but that's the problem right there. Serial multitaskers have to spend so much of their most valuable resources focused on the juggling aspect that they fail to progress or complete anything of substance.

Guy Winch, PhD and author of the book *"Emotional First Aid: Practical Strategies for Treating Failure, Rejection, Guilt, and Other Everyday Psychological Injuries"* explains that we never multitask in the real sense of the word. What we actually do from a cognitive perspective is task-switch. The problem with the task-switching process is the associated cost in time, effort and focus that's needed for the brain to realign between different tasks. It's this constant switching process that occurs when managing multiple tasks that causes our diminished productivity. What's more concerning though is that these detrimental effects are cumulative.

Over time it has been estimated that we can lose up to 40% of our cognitive power through the inefficiencies of task-switching. A lack of dedicated focus is quite literally draining your brain power, attention and ability to perform. If you want a quick demonstration of how your brain likes to work and the reason why multitasking is so ineffective, try this simple exercise:

In your mind, focus on the low-level details of carrying out any task or activity. Whilst playing through each detail try to focus and think about a second task or activity in the same way. If you do this correctly you will quickly discover that it's impossible to consciously think about and focus on more than one thing at a time, yet that's exactly what we try and do when multitasking.

Remember how I talked about the type of people who spend all of their time caught in the busy being busy trap? Well that's the multitasker at work. The challenge facing the serial multitasker is that juggling or *"plate spinning"* as it's often referred to is not about completion, it's about maintaining a constant state of *"work in progress"* that's rarely, if ever, truly completed. Working in this way not only thwarts productivity, it means you will never achieve the expected results.

> **Startup Pro Insight:** It's a scientifically proven fact that the more tasks we take on, the more our attention, focus, standards and ability to complete quality work becomes

diluted. By multitasking we are actually killing our ability to be effective rather than increasing it.

Now I know that keeping focused is a lot easier said than done, especially for us entrepreneurs. Our nature is one of high energy, short attention spans and fleeting ideas, and as such we find it more difficult than most to focus on just one thing at a time. I have struggled with this myself in the past, and unfortunately there is no known cure for this tendency, it's built right into our entrepreneurial DNA. What you can do however is learn how to harness and manage those gifts effectively. Having a single focus strategy will not only accelerate your results but will also allow you to be more selective about your time and more importantly what you put into it.

To quickly highlight how productive you can be with a single focused mindset, I would like you to try this simple experiment. Set a timer for just one hour and focus on one piece of work or one task. Do not allow any interruptions or distractions and keep 100% of your attention focused on that specific task.

At the end of the hour have a quick rollcall of what you have completed. You will be amazed at just how much you will have achieved by focusing on *"the one thing"*. Don't take my word for it, just go and try it for a couple of hours. Even better try it for a day or two. Focus on completion before moving onto something new. You will not only realise just how much can be achieved in one day you will also quickly expose the raft of wastefulness that surreptitiously creeps in and steals your time and detracts your efforts. Both of which have limited daily supply.

Startup Pro Insight: Being singularly focused on one specific task is how the most wealthy and successful entrepreneurs get done in one month what others take six months or more to complete. Often this is enough of an advantage to turn a small opportunity into a massive success.

33

Don't Wait For Approval

Startup Pro Insight: Waiting for approval to get started is just another excuse for not getting out there and doing it.

Waiting for or asking for approval or permission is what followers do and is not the decisive behaviour of a leader. In addition to this, asking for approval often ends up with someone somewhere saying no, normally because they do not have the power to say yes themselves. I live by this simple motto:

It's far easier to seek forgiveness than it is to seek approval.

34

IT'S GOT TO BE PERFECT

Who told you that?

Success at anything is about time to develop, measure, learn and iteratively improve. There are no shortcuts to getting this right, and you almost certainly won't get it right the first, or even the second, time around. Your first product or service will be rough around the edges, it will have elements you don't like and know could be better, and you will be embarrassed and perhaps under confident about certain areas. All I can tell you on this point is this:

Accept it.

Once you do, your life will be happier, less stressful and it will be far easier to gain a clear view of what's really important. Many new entrepreneurs start a business under the misguided belief that everything in the world has to be perfect before they can launch. The trouble with this approach is that it gets you stuck in the rut of wanting, and more importantly believing that you need, perfect products, perfect services, perfect marketing, killer websites or that the latest social marketing whiz is SEO optimised to the max before you can launch.

The reality for successful entrepreneurs of course is very different. How many times have well-known software vendors released a product that's so far from perfect it's barely fit for purpose?

As I keep reiterating, putting the icing on the cake can only happen once you have a cake, and even then it's only worth putting the icing on if the cake's worth eating. In other words, don't invest any more time developing or honing your product or service further than having a **Minimum Viable Product** to test. Remember your initial startup mission is not about a business or launching completely functional products and end-to-end services. Your objective at this point is simply to identify an audience with a problem, define solutions and devise experiments to prove and validate your early assumptions, that's it. Product and service development comes after you launch and not before.

> **Startup Pro Insight:** Perfection does not exist. It's largely subjective, and as such differs wildly in its interpretation. Spending time, money and effort trying to second guess what **"perfect"** may look like from your potential customers' perspective is at best completely ineffective, and at worst will have you running to the bankruptcy courts with your tail between your legs. Harsh but true.

35

MASTER THE 80/20 RULE

80% of success is mindset, 20% is application and execution

There are people out there who can do what you do. There may even be people out there who are capable of doing what you do and are far better at it than you. The thing is they will never achieve what you do because they don't have the correct mindset required to apply what they know in a way that delivers tangible value to others. That's an important distinction and one worth remembering.

Many can do, but few actually will do, the question is: which one are you?

Developing the right attitude and mindset will get you much further than the established expert who is unable to execute and implement his ideas. Your mindset not only governs what you think, importantly it also governs how you act, and how you act is the fundamental difference between the 20% who are successful and the 80% who will remain wannabes. Here are my top six tips for developing a winning mindset:

Believe in yourself first and foremost

Know that success is possible for you

Value yourself and what you know and understand how it is highly valuable to others

Raise your standards

Associate with those who are successful

Continual learning and self-education

Startup Pro Insight: Remember success at anything is 80% mindset and 20% mechanics. If you have it the other way around you're going to have a really tough time being successful.

36

LEARN WHILE YOU EARN

It's a popular misconception that you have to be a guru or subject matter expert to add extraordinary value and become amazingly successful. As I have already said, there is no such thing as perfection and if you wait for it you will see the best opportunities pass you by.

You really don't need to try and know everything about a subject before you can start providing huge value to others. Anyone who knows me well will tell you that when I get an idea all I do is get the bare basics down and then start learning about what needs to be done and then go and do it. The rest, well I learn that as I go. I have developed a number of business interests across a diverse range of industries, but not knowing an industry intimately has never stopped me from leveraging an opportunity when I saw it. I have just got good at learning what I need to know right now to get started and then executing quickly. Sometimes learning to distil down exactly what's needed now alongside the ability to execute quickly can be the biggest competitive advantage out there.

> **Startup Pro Insight:** The best way of learning anything is by doing it, no shortcuts, no magic or secrets, just plain old-fashioned hard graft.

37

THE HIDDEN ACCELERATOR

You may not always have the knowledge and skills needed to leverage an opportunity personally, however that should never prevent you from being able to add value and solve problems. Remember value does not always need to come from you directly to solve problems effectively. Knowing where to find it and facilitating its application however is a real entrepreneurial skill well worth mastering. Today, it's easy to tap into valuable sources of information, experience, knowledge and expertise that we have available to us via our acquaintances, friends, colleagues and networks. Now don't get me wrong, you cannot bluff your way into brain surgery - although someone has probably already tried and may even be doing it as we speak. A worrying thought I think you'll agree? What I'm saying is that you don't have to be limited in what you can achieve based upon the knowledge, skills and expertise that you have today. What's really interesting about the most wily and resourceful entrepreneurs is they are masters at two things:

They actively embrace continual learning and self-education.

They are experts at leveraging and utilising the skills, expertise, and knowledge of those around them as quickly and as effectively as possible. It's an essential skill and one of the best ways of quickly creating, building and launching new ventures.

Don't underestimate the value held within your network. Most people under-value and under-utilise their networks, merely using them for social interactions. On several occasions I have tipped the balance in my favour and won consulting projects because my contacts and alumni have been just as important and as valuable as my own personal knowledge and experience. My advice is don't fall foul of the debilitating misconception that you need to know everything before you can deliver value to your customers.

One of the things that we all tend to be bad at is asking for help. Interestingly enough when you ask for help something amazing happens, you tend to get it by the bucket load. Most people are more than happy to chip in when asked, especially if it involves them in something new and exciting or where they can openly demonstrate their own prowess and expertise.

> Einstein famously said, "never try and remember anything you can look up", and in today's connected world that's easier than ever to achieve.

You cannot know everything, but knowing to who and where you can go to attain the knowledge, skills and help you need, when you need it, is often as valuable as any knowledge or skill that you currently possess.

38

LAZINESS, THE HIDDEN ASSET

Startup Pro Insight: When I have defined the tasks and skills needed to achieve any goal my first thoughts are: "Who can help me get this done quicker, cheaper and more effectively than I can achieve on my own?"

By default, most of us try to do everything ourselves, or if not everything then certainly more than we really should do. It's inherent in our nature to be as independent and self-sufficient as possible. We look upon enlisting help as a failure at some level. This however is not the mindset of successful entrepreneurs and one you need to quickly change if you want to work smarter rather than harder. I have found this a challenge myself from time to time, but have learned that trying to do everything myself takes a lot more work, time and effort and can often end up with the results not being as good as they could have been if I had only asked for help. Whenever you undertake a new project or venture one of the first things you should be asking yourself is this:

"Who do I know within my network who would be willing to help me or could personally introduce me to others with the skills I need?"

You have the Internet, social networks, forums, niche groups, in fact a wealth of knowledge and experience literally at your fingertips and all you need do is ask. The reason why this is so powerful is because it provides you with the leverage to achieve things you simply could not do on your own. Many new entrepreneurs tend to work in isolation and fail to leverage their networks and associated resource pools effectively, simply because they do not think or want to ask for help

Ever heard this? *"Seek and ye shall find"*. In other words, if you ask you shall receive. The bottom line here is that people love to help. They love to discuss and talk about what interests them, what they are good at and of their achievements. Most of all though they love to contribute.

I often ask for help and can only remember being turned down twice, but the information, help and assistance I have received from those who freely gave their time and knowledge has been invaluable to me over the years. So asking someone to help you who can make your life easier, help you avoid lengthy and costly mistakes, and help you get things done quickly should be top of your startup to do list.

> **Startup Pro Insight:** It's important to note though that you must be prepared to pay this help and assistance forward at some point. Success has a habit of coming around and you may well be the one being asked to help in future

39

STAND UP & STAND OUT

How do you stand out from the crowd?

Imagine you go into a DIY store and you're buying nails. When you get to the nails you see that they are all the same size, colour, quality and price.

So the question is:

"Which one do you buy?"

The answer is of course:

"The first one that you come to."

Why?

Because there's no differentiation, no advantage and no reason to buy one particular nail over another.

Conversely, I like to think of myself as the sparkling nail that meets and greets the prospective customer at the door, adds immediate value, solves their problem quickly and efficiently and is marching them out of the door as happy customers long before they even get a chance to see the other nails, let alone giving them the opportunity to deliver a pitch. Your aim is to stand out so much that your competition becomes insignificant by comparison. So looking at that analogy how do you differentiate yourself and the value you deliver to stand out from the crowd?

Fortunately, that's really simple. Unfortunately, it's not easy. You're going to need to roll your sleeves up and do some work here. Let me give you an example of how I am the only nail worth choosing from my customers' perspective in my chosen field of change and transformation. Firstly, and most importantly, my clients come to me. This normally occurs through invitation and recommendation only. I don't waste my time sending impersonal spammy emails. I don't offer cheap gimmicky freebies or go knocking on every door in the neighbourhood cold calling to SELL. That approach is not only time consuming, it's hard work and way too much effort. I work on the following simple principles:

> **Always put yourself in your clients' shoes** - Would you buy from you and why, or more importantly why not?

> **The more effective your marketing the less you have to sell** - You should be looking to develop marketing systems and campaigns that create awareness, build traffic, create leads and convert them to sales. Automating the grunt work and qualifying leads on autopilot is one of the most effective ways of developing a **"pull"** rather than a traditional **"push"** marketing strategy.

> **Generate emotion -** The more emotion you can create in your clients' eyes, the more interest, urgency and propensity to buy you will generate. Tapping into emotions is one of the most effective marketing strategies to leverage.

Don't sell, serve - Forget selling, people hate to be sold to. Help, serve, and educate whilst providing as much actionable and demonstrable value as you can.

Create demand - I have already mentioned this tactic elsewhere but it's worth a second mention in case you missed it. **Creating demand for your clients is much more effective than waiting for them to create it for themselves.** Creating the demand in your customers' minds will allow you to quickly build interest, create new customers, grow revenues and close sales any time you like.

Reduce uncertainty - Everyone hates uncertainty and the more uncertain your prospective clients are about you, your product and your company, the less they will want to interact with and buy from you. Reducing uncertainty within these areas is a sure-fire way of building trust, promoting your position and increasing sales.

This Is How I Stand Out From The Crowd.

Many people believe that standing out from the crowd means having to produce breakthrough innovations, create disruptive technologies, redefine entire industries or literally reinvent the wheel to be successful. Whilst that can help of course, most of us out there building businesses have to rely on softer innovations to give us an edge. Here is a quick overview of how I stand out from the crowd with my consulting and coaching clients. Remember this is the approach that works for me. Your approach may need to be very different depending upon your circumstances, industry and proposition. What follows is an example of how you can start creating clients that's not reliant upon the old, outdated and ineffective methods that everyone else is using.

Before a potential client or customer approaches me with a work brief, they will have already validated my position in the marketplace. They can do this because I have developed a *"multi-presence"* strategy. Multi-presence is simply a holistic ecosystem of marketing and promotional resources including online presence, interviews, podcasts, social media, tools, publications, recommendations and testimonials that build customer awareness of my brand, position me as the expert, and generate interest.

These resources not only validate my credentials as the *"go to expert"* in my chosen field but also build pre-sales credibility, confidence and trust which in turn ensures that my prospective customers and clients are pre-qualified before they even contact me. In many cases I get potential clients to complete a simple online questionnaire that qualifies them even further. I also freely communicate my availability and pricing. Communicating pricing up front is counterintuitive to what many traditional marketing methods dictate, but it means that by the time a prospective customer engages with me they are completely pre-sold on my solutions, know what I can do for them and are aware of my pricing. Upfront price awareness is important to the way I work because it ensures that the investment (notice I said investment and not cost) required is never the sticking point or one of early negotiation. This approach guarantees that the initial conversations are based upon important metrics such as key objectives, required outcomes and desired results. In short, the focus is on what value will be delivered, why it matters to the client and demonstrates how working with me will improve their condition. Building client relationships in this way is far more effective than the traditional push and persuasion marketing methods that many are using. Being selective about who you work with will allow you to do the following:

Require far fewer clients

Minimise your marketing efforts

Maintain the highest possible standards

Build a premium brand

Serve your clients better than anyone else

Charge higher fees

Deliver far more meaningful value

Allow you to work alongside the best and most exciting clients

Don't forget, positioning is everything. You are the one who can provide solutions to their problems and improve their condition. In short, everything that you do should communicate to your prospective customers that they are dealing with a respected professional, the best in the business and a true industry expert who knows exactly how to ease their pain, help them overcome their most critical challenges and facilitate their progress in some way.

The second way of standing out is to take Seth Godin's excellent advice and build *"purple cows"*. That is to make sure that your product and your service is remarkable in some way. My remarkable **"stand out"** differentiator is that I have developed and built a unique proprietary framework, approach and toolset that helps businesses to develop their capability to successfully lead, manage, support and deliver innovation, change and transformation across their enterprises. This, alongside a disruptive pricing and delivery model, has secured my *"expert position"* in this area. No one else has done or is doing anything like it and it's my *"purple cow'* or what makes me the *"go to"* person for change and transformation advice and guidance.

So what do you need to do exactly to build credibility trust and confidence as the "go to" industry expert?

Personally, I carry out a number of activities which include; book writing, guest posts, and publishing thought provoking articles and commentary. I provide easy access to exclusive content, videos, podcasts and training materials. I'm active on a number of industry forums, have testimonials, speak at major industry events and am on the advisory panel of several large organisations.

Developing a multi-presence approach not only develops brand awareness and credibility from a buyer's perspective but also builds the trust and confidence that paves the way to mutually beneficial relationships. A secondary advantage of multi-presence is the ease with which you can demonstrate your value and what it would be like to work with you in future. Demonstrating your value is extremely important here because it erodes and filters out much of the grey, mediocre *"also ran"* competition. Remember the nails?

> The difference between my competitors and me is this. Most talk about how good they are. I can prove it.

I am not suggesting that you will need all of these credibility building elements all at once to be successful, it has taken me a considerable time to build up these resources, tools and assets. The topics discussed are merely a few ideas and suggestions to help you get started on developing and building a robust marketing approach that works for you.

40

DELIVER ON THE PROMISE

Just deliver outstanding value and the rest will follow

The world has become completely desensitised to the cheap and mediocre. Average has become the default from the food we eat, to the service we get, to the quality of the products we buy. This however represents the perfect opportunity for the savvy entrepreneur.

Why?

Because it presents a great opportunity to stand out from the crowd before you have even got started. On a number of occasions I have won a deal just for turning up, looking the part and providing some small recommendations, insights or advice that my *"soon to be"* client found extremely valuable. The chances are that everyone else up to that point had been selling rather than serving. This approach quickly builds the kind of credibility, trust and instant emotional rapport that has my new clients literally signing me up as I'm walking out of the door.

The fact is that it's really simple to look like a knight in shining armour when everyone else around you looks so bland, uninteresting and average. In virtually every single industry every *"nail"* is the same as every other *"out of the box"* commodity nail with no differentiation, no remarkability and more importantly no reason to do business with.

> **Startup Pro Insight:** No one wants to hire or buy average when excellence is available just around the corner.

The old adage of under promise and over deliver is king here. This is where delivering far in excess of the expectation not only positions you on top of the pile it automatically qualifies you to get rewarded accordingly.

> **Startup Pro Insight:** Your job as an entrepreneur is to deliver outstanding value and service that your clients will find irresistible and, even better, irreplaceable. You will never have to sell again if you work at getting this right. I never ever sell to a client, I have helped hundreds instantly recognise my value though.

41

TAKE YOUR SEAT AT THE TABLE

You have probably heard this saying a million times: You need to be in it to win it."

That makes perfect sense doesn't it? But you would be amazed by how many people don't get it. In fact I'm slightly embarrassed about pointing this out, but I am going to do it all the same.

If you're doing nothing, guess what you're going to get?

Sitting on the side-lines being an armchair entrepreneur is not going to work.

Gaining sales without making offers is not going to work.

Getting people to connect with you if you don't reach out to them is not going to work.

No one will know you exist if you don't promote how you can help them.

Get out there, talk to people, help them, educate them, hustle them, and yes, clients do need to be hustled and directed a little from time to time. Now that bit for me is where the buzz, excitement and interest really is. I love doing deals, I love the hustle or rainmaking as it's often referred to, and that's what makes great entrepreneurs great. You may not be comfortable with becoming a rainmaker on day one, or even day one hundred and one, but you're going to need to learn to love it because once you can make rain anything's possible.

42

VALUE YOUR TIME

Value your time, because no one else will. Most people carelessly waste, discard and undervalue their time in the misguided belief that tomorrow always comes and supply is endless.

> Everyone knows you get a whole load more time tomorrow, right?

Let me tell you right now that time is your most valuable resource, and should be treated like the gold that it is. As with anything of value you need to learn how to use it, invest it and manage it wisely to make it work for you and deliver as much value as possible.

> **Startup Pro Insight:** Unlike money, which is in abundance and can be easily replaced, you do not have the same luxury with your time. Once it has been spent that's it, you never get it back. Yes, you may get more tomorrow (if you're lucky) but your supply is finite and most definitely limited. Treat it like gold and be judicious where you invest it.

> "I have never met a wealthy successful person who didn't value time above all else. Conversely, I have never met a poor person who did." - James Kingham

43

LEVERAGE YOUR IP

Startup Pro Insight: What you know, what you do and how you do it and your ability to translate those skills into a value proposition has a direct correlation to your capability to generate revenue.

The skills, knowledge and experiences that you have accumulated over time are like the raw ingredients of a cake. Individually they provide a small amount of standalone value, but learn how to blend them effectively, bake them well and present them to *"perceived"* perfection however and you will have a recipe worth a fortune. Think about your skills, what you know, what you do and how that could be packaged up into products and services that solve problems and create value for others.

The thing is, we all know much more than we think we do. The problem is that we take much of what we know for granted, and in doing so we dismiss the incredible value it can hold for others. This is one of the biggest mistakes that new entrepreneurs make. Your gained knowledge, experiences, insights and expertise have high intellectual property value and as such can be developed into uniquely valuable assets that can be leveraged for profit.

No matter who you are or what you do I will guarantee that you will have hidden gems of wisdom that could be defined and packaged up into a range of highly valuable products or services with little effort. Once you have that nailed it's simply a case of defining your *"interested audience"* and figuring out the best methods of reaching them and helping them apply that value in a meaningful way.

I'm going to prove to you right now that your idle ideas, knowledge and expertise are worth a fortune. Go and grab a pen and piece of A4 paper, it's ok I will wait. Now divide the page into three columns. In column one list all of the skills, knowledge and expertise that you have. Make sure you include everything, no matter how small. In the second column list the benefits of that knowledge, what it provides and value it could deliver. In the third column list all the types of people or organisations where the value listed in column two could be leveraged and how this could be multiplied many times over if you simply packaged that value up into a defined product or service. Take a long hard look at the list and now tell you me you don't value what you know. The piece of paper in front of you right now is a **business blueprint worth a fortune**. This is an exercise that I get my **"on the side" startup pro** course attendees to do and the results are astonishing. If you have not done it yet, just invest fifteen minutes of your time to get it all down on paper. You will be amazed at just how much you know and the value it could be delivering to others.

> **Startup Pro Insight:** Never underestimate what you know and the value it holds and creates for others. Remember a client's problem will always be a problem because they do not possess the **"know how"** to solve it themselves. All you

need to do to create massive value is shine the light and show them the way forward. Remember the bigger the problem, the bigger the reward.

44

CUSTOMER CREATION

One of the most common problems for new startups is this. You're excited and revved up about your new business, you love your products and services, you're filling a niche and are fantastic at what you do. The problem is you have no customers, and getting them appears to be some kind of dark art secret that no one is willing to share with you. Sound familiar?

Before we delve into the detail I want to clarify a couple of things. Firstly, customers and clients are not acquired, won or attracted, they are created. And you do not create customers by sending them mountains of faceless impersonal emails, broadcasting endless social media messages, sharing pictures, writing blogs and articles, or speaking at events, that's marketing. While all of those methods are valid for demonstrating value and building brand awareness, they do not create customers in isolation. People buy from people, and people are all about relationships. You are, or need to be, in the *"relationship business"*.

What I am about to share with you here is a pragmatic, common-sense approach for quickly creating customers. Whist there are many different ways of creating customers I am going to focus on one particular aspect here simply because it's the most effective, especially if you are starting from scratch. Most small businesses and solo entrepreneurs spend a considerable amount of time, effort and money trying to directly create customers themselves. Whilst this is of course the ideal scenario it's definitely not the most effective way to do it when you're starting from scratch. After much trial and error, I discovered that the best way to reach my target audience was to focus my efforts on developing relationships with those organisations that were already serving my target audience.

In my case I provide a range of professional consulting services to businesses who need to build their capability to successfully lead, manage, support and deliver change and transformation across their organisations. Most of my target audience are focusing on transformation to increase customer value and drive competitive advantage. I made the decision early on to channel my consulting services through organisations that already had customers who were investing in technology solutions. In many instances these same customers had a direct need for assistance in helping them navigate the complexities of business and organisational change and transformation. I started developing my existing relationships with IT service providers and vendors whilst identifying other businesses who I could develop mutually beneficial partnerships and joint ventures with. Initially I had three propositions.

> **Service Integration** - The service provider or vendor simply bolted on my professional service catalogue to their existing services portfolio. This immediately augmented their own capability to expand market reach and increases sales opportunities with existing clients. I would either work

under their name and reputation or under my own banner dependent upon the service provider's business model and requirements. Profit to the service provider would be derived from a commission-based model or a wholesale purchase of consulting services and packages that could be drawn down during a given time period. This simple approach provided valuable new services with good profit potential, and little effort, investment or ongoing maintenance being required from the service provider.

Channel Partner - In this scenario, the service provider would not only use my services as a direct value-add proposition for their existing clients, they would actively market and sell my services through their business as an approved partner and in doing so would be able to target and develop completely new market opportunities that they would not have been able to serve on their own.

Reseller - The simplest model and ideal for ad-hoc obligation free arrangements. Service providers would recommend my services on an ad-hoc basis. This model worked well where a service provider did not want to add additional services outside of their core business model or undertake a joint venture arrangement, but saw the potential to occasionally add value to their clients via a recommendation or referral. Any work would be undertaken on a straight commission basis.

From a *"standing start"* perspective these types of partner and joint venture arrangements worked well. They were easy to propose and added real value and profit potential from the partner's perspective. Within a short time I had created a small robust network of active partners and an ongoing pipeline of high-value consulting clients. This model allowed me to go from a standing start to creating significant revenues very quickly and with minimal marketing effort needed on my part.

If you need to quickly create customers early on, my advice is to identify those who have direct trusted access to your interested audience and then develop ways to present your offerings as non-competing complementary services that deliver equitable value to you, your joint venture partner and the clients. I like to look at it this way. It's a lot easier to work with just a handful of established organisations who are already serving your audience than it is to try and build completely new sales pipelines from scratch yourself. Whilst this type of channel or distribution model does not work for every type of business, service or product, it's definitely a quick, effective way of building momentum and traction early on.

During the early startup stages I would suggest that 70% of your business should be coming through your joint venture partnerships, with 30% being created directly. This model is a good compromise between building your own direct customer relationships, gaining traction and generating early revenue. I have known businesses who have worked with just one or two joint venture partners for their entire revenue stream. Whilst this may appear to be an attractive proposition it can be a risky long-term strategy. I have seen a number of businesses go under or struggle financially where markets or businesses change or hit hardships. Spreading your sales pipeline across a diverse range of channels serves best and is a much more robust approach in the longer-term.

It's worth noting that whilst joint ventures, partnerships and affiliations may take a chunk of profit out of your bottom line, the exposure to highly qualified customers is a worthwhile trade. As I have already said, this method is ideal for gaining quick early traction with the option to then develop your own more profitable pipelines once you have reached adequate revenue, income and profit sufficiency levels. It's a good idea to build the partnership consideration into your early financial models if this is the way you wish to go. Doing so will ensure that you have a feasible commercial model that provides enough financial incentive to make it compelling from your channel partner's perspective, whilst still maintaining a decent level of income and profitability from your side.

Two questions I get asked frequently are.

"How much commission should I pay partners?" and "What type of percentage is compelling from a partner's point of view?"

The answer is, it depends.

Your industry, business model, products and services will vary widely, but keep in mind that your commission rates will need to be attractive enough for the partner to invest time and effort in actively selling your services. In the field of professional consulting services I normally pay between 10-12.5% commissions for ad-hoc recommendations that result in work and circa 15-25% for qualified partners who are actively promoting and selling services on my behalf. The percentage variance takes into consideration work volume, frequency and payment terms.

45

BOOSTING PRODUCTIVITY

Much has been written about productivity, what it is, how it works and how you can become better at it. I like to keep things simple, so for me productivity is about how quickly and efficiently I can get my most important and significant work completed.

Productivity has become an enigma to many, but in fact the main reason why some people are more productive than others is simply down to commitment, discipline and focus, as discussed in an earlier chapter.

Two of the biggest productivity killers are:

Taking on way too much.

Taking on way too much of what does not count.

It's not that we are necessarily unproductive, it is just that we become focused on the wrong things at the wrong time and for the wrong reasons. Increased productivity needs order and discipline to clearly identify the most valuable work. Once you have identified your most valuable work you need to then apply urgency and commitment to that work in order to deliver results as quickly as possible. Your outcomes and results by the way should always be both progressive and measurable in some way. It's important to clarify how productivity should be measured. In my eyes a measure of productivity is not, as many believe, in the number of tasks completed, but in the level of progress made and measurable results delivered.

Take a minute to think about how many distractions you have around you right now. Your phone, the Internet, social media, emails, pointless meetings and wayward conversations for example. As you will no doubt have gathered by now I like to keep things quick, small and simple and never have more than three priority things to get completed in one day.

The reason I define just three daily priorities is simple. If you have more three defined outcomes on your priority to do list, I'm afraid you don't have priorities at all. What you have is a wish list. I have developed a simple way to prioritise my workload and it starts with a single question:

What work is going to provide me with the most progress towards reaching my most important objectives, outcomes and measurable results?

Anything that is not progressing your ability to meet an important strategy aligned milestone or goal is wasted effort.

46

TURNING ON THE AUTOPILOT

The less time you need to spend working on low-level commodity tasks the better. The aim here is to ensure that you're spending the majority of your time focused on your most important and valuable work. Work which delivers measurable progress in some way.

To ensure that you maintain a razor-sharp focus on the *"big"* stuff, you need to adopt and apply a *"lean"* mindset to what you do, how you do it and, most importantly, when. Taking the time to evaluate *"what you do"*, *"how"* **and** *"when"* can provide valuable insights into the actual *"time"* cost alongside the value that's being delivered as a result.

Identifying laborious time-consuming commodity tasks that can be quickly reorganised, automated or outsourced to release your time can pay dividends in the long run. Remember the aim here is to reduce the need for you to be involved in the day-to-day **"doing"** of manual intensive tasks. This becomes even more pertinent if these tasks occur on a regular basis and are repeatable in nature. The name of the game here is to release as much of your most precious resource (time) as possible so that you can focus on the work that only you can do and delivers the biggest results.

Startup Pro Insight: If you're always busy but achieving or delivering little, the chances are you have become fixated on work that **"appears"** to be important rather than identifying the work that's **"essential"** to progress. The fact is that most of us find it hard to prioritise the most valuable work because we often become more focused on the completion of tasks rather than progression of results. The easy way to identify and prioritise your most important work is to ask these two simple questions:

Does the work I am doing make progress towards a clearly identified goal that delivers a clear result aligned to the achievement of my objectives and strategies?

Does completing this work directly deliver a tangible result or is it a longer-term dependency for another piece of work?

By default, larger workloads generate high numbers of dependencies that can eat time and deliver little. It's really important to balance **"quick wins"** alongside longer-term dependent work. Don't fall into the trap of focusing on the wrong work at the wrong time.

Converting manual tasks and workloads to fully automated *"hands off"* processes is a really simple concept but it's often a challenging one for many to master well. The truth is that most people never learn to prioritise and master time effectively and end up with time becoming the master of them. This common misalignment inevitably leads to a loss of performance, missed opportunities, longer and longer working days and ever reducing results. Getting yourself into a position where you can minimise your time input is not only important, it's absolutely essential to enable you to leverage and maximise your efforts.

Many of the people that I coach and mentor find themselves continually *"plate spinning"* or *"treading water"*. That's to say they spend most of their time as busy administrators of tasks rather than focusing on outcomes and results. The end is always the same. Progress stalls, performance suffers, and they end up achieving little alongside excessive time and effort expenditure.

How often do you hear others saying things like, **"I'm so busy but just don't seem to be getting anything done"** or **"I'm rushed off my feet"**, that's the busy task administrator at work. This scenario is often the end result of saying *"yes"* to everything, lost focus and an inability to prioritise effectively.

Why would you think that it's productive to reinvent the wheel every time you do something?

We often wrongly believe that we need to *"reinvent the wheel"* whenever we do something, in order for it to be valuable. This is a key differentiator between the wannapreneur and the true thoroughbred entrepreneur. Wannapreneurs feel they have to do it all themselves and from the ground up to make it count. Entrepreneurs on the other hand are masters at finding the quickest route to getting anything done. Real entrepreneurs would rather tread well-known paths, stand on the shoulders of giants and build upon the experiences and successes of others than struggle to build from the ground up every time.

If what you need to achieve, build or use has already been done, use it and spend the saved time, effort and money figuring out the best ways to add a unique twist, that's a much better use of time. In short, it's ok to be lazy, where it matters. The trouble with us humans is that we have an insatiable need to feel we are contributing in some way. Contribution is one of our most basic needs and desires. This need outwardly manifests itself with us trying to apply, or more accurately to **contribute**, our knowledge, experiences and beliefs to the *"problem to be solved"*. This automated cognitive response of leveraging *"what we know"* is fantastic and helps us in many situations, but being productive and getting things done quickly is not one of them.

The power of the brain is truly incredible. When faced with new challenges it automatically tries to use our internal reference models to quickly find answers to our problems. This activity is largely based upon our knowledge, experiences and data gathered from outcomes we have experienced in the past. Our brains use this information to interpret and compare similar scenarios already held on *"file"*, so to speak. This is the brain's way of quickly assessing a situation and then applying *"best"* known logic to quickly and decisively make decisions about what action should be taken to attain the best result or define available options to take.

One of the best ways to become highly productive is to use and feed this area of the brain by building up mental references, templates and blueprints and then consciously grouping things together that look similar in nature and type so that they may be recalled and applied to new scenarios as they occur. This is a proven methodology and highly valuable in becoming more effective at decision making and enhancing day-to-day productivity.

47

SCALING YOUR INCOME

Regardless of industry, business type or value provided, your time is not scalable which in turn significantly limits your income potential. Yes, you can work longer hours or increase your prices or fees, but it's all finite. The most effective way of increasing your earning capacity to virtually limitless levels is to start developing opportunities that create income passively.

High Passive Income Profitability (HPIP)

HPIP is a lean-based principle that I have developed and use regularly to identify areas where reorganisation, automation and outsourcing can effectively remove manual processes from the income earning process. Removing yourself and the reliance upon your time as the primary income source is one of the most fundamental wealth creation principles for developing passive or near passive income potential. We all have 24 hours a day to invest, but the key difference between the most successful and productive people and everyone else is how smartly they invest that time. Ok, so we're agreed, we all have 24 hours a day to work with. It would make perfect sense therefore to develop the capability to remove yourself as a dependency from the income generation process and free up as much of your time as possible to invest in work that **produces** rather than **consumes**.

Identifying opportunities to optimise your time rather than consuming it is the key differentiation between limited time-bound revenue generation and scalable **High Passive Income Profitability (HPIP).**

> **Startup Pro Insight:** Remember, your time is not scalable. The only way to effectively scale your time is to undertake the work that ONLY you can do. Everything else should be organised, automated or outsourced. The best and most productive entrepreneurs are those who become highly skilled at identifying opportunities to save and multiply time rather than consume it.

The importance of developing a mindset based upon passivity is one of the core Quick, Small and Simple micro startup principles. Once you have developed and honed this simple formula you will be able to quickly distil your most important, significant and urgent work into the component parts that drive rapid productivity increases.

HPIP has a number of domain components that work well and produce great results in isolation but when combined produce a powerful productivity ecosystem that's worth way more than the sum of its parts.

The HPIP formula for scaling time and productivity

HPIP works on the premise of reducing areas of waste and inefficiency whilst accelerating areas where productivity and passivity can be leveraged.

Areas of Reduction

Getting organised, Reducing wastage, Systemise and standardise processes

Areas of Acceleration

Outsourcing, Automation, Duplication, Multiplication

Areas Of Reduction

Organise

Taking the time to organise your workload is a key component of being able to ensure that you're focusing on the most important, significant and urgent work. Being able to define your most productive work is important because it also allows you to reduce wasted effort on otherwise low-level insignificant work whilst freeing up valuable resources that can be invested more wisely elsewhere. You will notice that I reference time and effort as investments and I do so by design. If you look at your time and effort in the same vein as money, in that they are all valuable resources that can be used for investment and subsequent return, you will quickly develop a mindset focused on investment and subsequent returns. The result of the organisation process is to identify three core types of work:

Work that only you can do and delivers clear progress towards a defined outcome - This may mean using your proprietary knowledge to design and develop your intellectual property or your service or product.

Work that can be fully automated – This may be work like sales and marketing campaigns, product or service delivery or customer feedback.

Work that can be delegated or outsourced to others – This may include work like software development, book writing, administration via a virtual assistance or customer support for example.

Identifying & Removing Wastage

Monitoring what you do, how you do it and the frequency is important. It's important because it's really easy to lose sight of what you actually do on a day-to-day basis when you're down in the weeds doing it. Being able to take a step back and identify highly labour-intensive tasks and associated wastage that can be removed, automated, outsourced or delegated is an essential part of becoming really productive. I have several simple qualifying questions I ask myself about the tasks and workload I undertake:

Why am I doing this work?

Why does it matter?

What is the measurable value?

Is this work wasted effort or have little or no measurable value?

Could someone else or an automated process be completing this work?

The aim here is simple. Identify and remove repeatable mundane tasks where personal involvement is required. Remember the requirement here is to reduce your workload and mitigate your personal input as much as possible or remove it completely if you can.

> **Startup Pro Insight:** Remember, **THE** best way of conserving your most valuable resources (time and effort) is not to have to spend them in the first place.

Standardisation

Standardising, templating and blueprinting are key elements for rapidly accelerating your productivity and scaling your time. They are also essential components to have in place when you're looking to delegate or outsource work to others. If you have a standardised approach that's repeatable, then it becomes very easy for others to follow what you do whilst maintaining quality and the predictability of results. The level of standardisation achieved will of course depend upon your business, operating model and services types, but some examples of standardisation might include templated forms, checklists, visual procedure guides, and standard blueprints for workflows and working practices. Standardisation may also encompass the complete manufacture and production processes of products. This may also include packing procedures, logistics and elements of distribution and sales. Standardisation should run through your entire value delivery chain from ideation through to delivery, support and feedback.

Areas Of Acceleration

Outsourcing & Delegating

I use the term outsourcing as a generic phrase that covers any work that you can effectively contract out to others, which equally includes delegation. Whilst delegation and outsourcing may look similar, they do have subtle but important differences. Delegation normally refers to work passed to individuals or teams within an organisation. Outsourcing on the other hand normally refers to work passed to outside third-party organisations for completion. Outsourcing is the third stage of the **HPIP** process and comes once you have identified the workload that could be carried out by others rather than yourself, reduced wastage and inefficiencies and standardised your processes and procedures.

My default position is to delegate and outsource as much as possible. In fact some of my own micro businesses are completely outsourced and automated, and as such require little or no day-to-day interaction, involvement or attention on my part other than overseeing the various operations. Although delegation and outsourcing can be one of the most liberating and necessary stages for scaling your business operations, especially if you are a one-man band or small organisation, it can also prove to be one of the hardest to achieve. It's hard to achieve for a number of reasons:

Most of us find it difficult to delegate and outsource because it's difficult to let go and feels somehow as though we are giving up control in some way.

Psychologically you may believe that you are absolutely essential to the success of your enterprise and you are the only one who can do the work to the required standard.

What you have to try and remember here is that you're trying to make yourself as expendable as possible, in fact in an ideal world you want to be completely redundant. Whether you manage to outsource and delegate effectively or not the fact remains, you simply cannot scale if you are the sole resource pool within your business and success relies upon your efforts, time and input to survive.

Automation

Now that you have cleared out the wastage, optimised what you do and standardised your approach, it's time to turn up the heat and start the transition from high overhead manual hand cranking to automated autopilot. Realistically you may not be in a position to remove, outsource and automate everything in one go, and in any case automation should be looked upon as ongoing evolution consisting of continuous and iterative improvement over time.

Most of the companies that I work with have been automating systems, processes and operational areas for years and will likely continue to do so well into the future. Automation is a crucial part of sustainable revenue generation and competitive advantage and bringing it all together is when the magic starts to happen.

Areas that can be automated vary dramatically from business to business but as a rule the following areas are ripe for automation for just about any business. As it happens they are also often the most important.

Production, Sales, Marketing, Order fulfilment, Training, Education, Product delivery, Support, Customer feedback

Remember, anything that you can automate is free time that can be invested elsewhere. As you will have no doubt realised by now, a massive part of success is not just about what you do, it's about the low-level mechanics of how and when you do it. Removing the reliance for your own time to be invested to generate revenue is one of the most effective strategies to learn, hone and master. It will allow you to maximise your effectiveness and productivity, and once mastered fully will allow you to extend your capability and capacity to focus on other projects without having to worry about your own personal time limitations. The idea in the long-term is that your most valuable work will be identifying opportunities, testing and validating your ideas and then focusing on implementing them and automating the income stream.

Multiplication

Once you have completed the other stages it's time to add the multiplication factor. This is where you can start to reap high productivity rewards. The multiplier effect from a startup's perspective is the stage where you can start distilling your entire startup process into a simple blueprint approach that can be templated and used again and again to easily, quickly and cost effectively launch highly profitable micro startups any time you wish.

Duplication

Like multiplication, taking the time to identify ways of duplicating your efforts without your direct input is a very valuable way of reducing your time and effort involvement. Coming up with systems and processes that can be easily duplicated, copied or cloned without your direct day-to-day input is a sure-fire way of seeing your revenues and profits soar.

Take a minute or two to think about what *"press button"* duplication capability would mean to your production, advertising, sales, marketing and fulfilment processes. What about the possibilities that franchising could offer? The whole premise of a successful franchise operation is a standardised system that can be duplicated and automatically multiplied at scale. Get duplication right and you can start to quickly extract yourself enough to be able to work on your business rather than in it.

> **Startup Pro Insight:** Resist (where possible) the urge to continually work in the business. Your role as an entrepreneur is to work on your businesses. Whilst that may be an old cliché, it's an old cliché for good reason. If you're working in your business you're really a freelancer or a long-term self-employed employee, who's permanently limited to exchanging time for money. True entrepreneurs leverage opportunities that free them from this limiting transactional constraint. This is the model used by the most successful entrepreneurs to grow their businesses, incomes and profits. I cannot stress enough the importance of extracting yourself as much as possible from your business and ensuring it does not become solely reliant upon you for its revenue. In order to progress you need to have enough time available to develop other interests, opportunities and income streams. If your chosen businesses need so much managing you may have inadvertently set yourself up in a job, have chosen the

wrong business model, or you need to drastically review your approach to revenue creation.

Get In Touch

James is an expert at helping people to develop multiple incomes by building and launching quick, small and simple **"On The Side"** startup projects. Visit the Online Startup Pro website today and discover how he can help you do the same.

james@onlinestartuppro.com

www.onlinestartuppro.com

© James Kingham 2019

How To Become A Startup Pro - On The Side 2016-2019

The Online Startup Pro © 2012-2019

Rights reserved. No part of this document may be reproduced in any form including photocopying or electronic transmission, without prior written consent of the author.

www.ingramcontent.com/pod-product-compliance
Lightning Source LLC
Chambersburg PA
CBHW020651220526
45464CB00001B/387